SPIRITUAL INTERVIEW WITH THE GUARDIAN SPIRIT OF
RODRIGO
DUTERTE

ドゥテルテ
フィリピン大統領
守護霊メッセージ

RYUHO OKAWA
大川隆法

序文

　最近来日されたフィリピンのドゥテルテ大統領がどういう人なのか。日本政府も、マスコミも、国際政治学者もさっぱり分からないらしい。ドゥテルテ氏の本心が分からなければ、日本も安全保障上のしっかりとした方針が出せず、アメリカ政府の顔色をうかがってばかり、といったことになりかねない。

　本書のドゥテルテ大統領の守護霊メッセージは、同時に彼の霊査(れいさ)(スピリチュアル・リーディング)もかねているので、"結論"がきわめて透明度の高いものとなっている。どうやら外見上、恐(こわ)そうなこの方の本心は、"日本の武士(さむらい)精神"のようである。彼の言動だけで先入観(せんにゅうかん)を持ちすぎず、日本国としては、フィリピン政府は信じられる、という態度をピシッと決めたらよいだろう。

Preface

Recently, the Philippines President Duterte visited Japan. What kind of a person is he? Even the Japanese government, the mass media, and the scholars of international politics don't work effectively. If we don't know the mindset of Mr. Duterte, Japan cannot establish a clear decision on national security, and will always be under the control of American government.

The messages from the guardian spirit of President Duterte in this book is quite clear. Because this is a spiritual reading on him. His appearance is like an old-fashioned "Father," but his true entity seems to be the "Japanese samurai spirit." Japan should be strongly determined to trust the Philippine government, without much prejudice on his sayings (and acts) only.

日本の真なる独立をも願っている、真なる愛国者の姿を発見して驚くのは、読者の楽しみとして期待してもらうこととしよう。

2016年11月3日
幸福の科学グループ創始者兼総裁
大川隆法

He wishes for Japan's true independence. I hope readers to be excited about the discovery of a true (samurai) patriot.

Nov. 3, 2016
Master and CEO of Happy Science Group
Ryuho Okawa

Contents

Preface 3

1 Looking through the Mind of the Mysterious President Duterte 20

2 Impression of the Visit to Japan and of Prime Minister Abe 26

The guardian spirit somehow knows about Japanese Shinto 26

Feeling very sorry about missing the meeting with the "god emperor" of Japan 34

The one word to describe Prime Minister Abe 38

3 "Just Kill Bad People" 46

The "open secret" of his success as mayor 46

"You need to pull off the bad tooth" 50

Same answer when asked about the future vision of the Philippines 58

4 How Does He See America and Japan as the God of the Philippines? 66

Officially a Catholic, but who is his God? 66

The truth about the voice of God he heard on the airplane 70

目　次

序文 2

1 「謎の人物」ドゥテルテ大統領の心を見抜く 21

2 訪日の感想と安倍首相の印象は？ 27
　　なぜか日本神道の知識があるドゥテルテ守護霊 27
　　「神」としての天皇陛下に会えず残念がる 35
　　安倍首相の印象は「一言(ひとこと)」に尽きる 39

3 「悪い奴らを殺すだけ」 47
　　市長時代に成功した理由は「公然の秘密」 47
　　「悪い歯は抜かないと駄目」 51
　　「フィリピンの未来ビジョン」を聞かれても一貫
　　した答え 59

4 「フィリピンの神」としてアメリカと日本を
　どう見るか 67
　　公式にはカトリック教徒だが、実際に信じている神
　　は誰か 67
　　「飛行機で聞いた神の声」の真相は？ 71

	His connection to Typhoon Haiyan that attacked the Philippines 76
	"Japan had to kill MacArthur at that time" 84

5 The Guardian Spirit Reveals His True Thinking on China 88

"We need Japan to protect weak countries of Asia" 88

The money from China is the rental fee of South China Sea? 94

He is just dealing with China to get money 100

"The United States and Great Britain should apologize to Asian people" 110

6 His Outlook on the South China Sea Problem with China 112

Both the Philippines and Japan must cut the leash 112

He wants to improve the safety in the Philippines and invite Japanese capitals 120

"We don't need to protect our sea" 126

7 The Guardian Spirit's Vision of the Asian Century 132

He is "the god of mercy inviting inferno for the United States" 132

フィリピンを襲った台風ハイエンとの関係 ……………… 77
　　「日本はあの時点でマッカーサーを殺すべきだった」 ……… 85

5　ドゥテルテ守護霊、中国に対する本心を明かす …… 89
　　「日本にアジアの弱い国々を守ってほしい」 ………………… 89
　　中国からの支援金は「南シナ海の〝レンタル料〟」？ ……… 95
　　中国とは、金をもらうために取り引きしているだけ ……… 101
　　米英はアジアの人々に謝罪すべき ……………………… 111

6　中国との南シナ海問題の見通しは？ ………………… 113
　　フィリピンも日本も「紐」を切らなければならない ……… 113
　　フィリピンの治安を良くして日本の資本を
　　招き入れたい ……………………………………………… 121

　　領海は「守らなくても大丈夫」？ ………………………… 127

7　「アジアの世紀」のビジョンを語る
　　ドゥテルテ守護霊 ………………………………………… 133
　　「アメリカに地獄をもたらす慈悲の神」を自称 …………… 133

"Trump will let Japan go as an Asian leader" 140

Suggesting Japanese as the official language of the new
Asian economic area 144

8 Revealing His Deep Connection to Japan and Speaking in Japanese 150

"I have a shrine in Japan" 150

A past life as a great general during Japan-China War and
Japan-Russia War 156

9 Regain the Spirit of Meiji and Stand Up, Japan 164

He complains about the emperor's abdication problem 164

Ill words are "to teach the samurai spirit to Japan" 172

Suggesting the Greater East Asia Co-Prosperity Sphere to
Japan from a foreign country 180

Advice for the Happiness Realization Party and Happy Science .. 182

10 Underground Plans for a New Worldview 188

"I will take as much as I can from China" 188

Reformers will come from Asian countries based on the
world plan by Happy Science 192

「トランプなら日本をアジアのリーダーにしてくれる」… 141
　「日本語を公用語とする新・アジア経済圏」を提唱 ………… 145

8　日本との「深い縁」を明かし、日本語で
　　語り始める …………………………………………………… 151
　「日本に私の神社がある」……………………………………… 151
　過去世は日清・日露戦争の、あの名将 ……………………… 157

9　日本は「明治の気概」を取り戻し立ち上がれ …… 165
　天皇の「生前退位」問題に苦言を呈する
　ドゥテルテ守護霊 ……………………………………………… 165
　暴言の真意は「日本に武士の気概を教えるため」………… 173
　外国から日本に「大東亜共栄圏」を提案している ………… 181
　幸福実現党と幸福の科学へのアドバイス …………………… 183

10　新たな世界観のための〝地下計画〟を語る
　　ドゥテルテ守護霊 …………………………………………… 189
　中国からは「むしるだけ、むしってやる」………………… 189
　幸福の科学の「世界計画」のもと、アジア各地に
　改革者が出てくる ……………………………………………… 193

End the "winning countries" system of the UN and make
a new worldview 198

Problems of the mass media in the Japanese election system
and in democracy 202

Heaven's plans to make China weaker 206

Comments on the Northern Territories issue with Russia 208

"I am one of the founding gods of Japan" 210

Why does he pretend to be uncivilized unlike his past life
as a great general? 216

11 After the Spiritual Interview from the Guardian
Spirit of Duterte 222

★ This spiritual interview was recorded in English until the first line of p.160, where the recording switched to Japanese from the second line onward. The Japanese text until the first line of p.160 is the translation of the English, and the English text from there onward is the translation of the Japanese.

国連の「戦勝国体質」を廃し、新たな世界観の構築を 199

日本の選挙システムや民主主義におけるマスコミ
の問題点 203

中国の「牙を抜く」天上界の計画とは 207

ロシアとの北方領土問題に関するコメント 209

日本の草創の神の一柱であることを明言 211

名将の生まれ変わりらしからぬ「野蛮な振る舞い」
は何のため？ 217

11　ドゥテルテ守護霊の霊言を終えて 223

※本書は、160ページ一行目までは英語で収録され、同二行目以降、日本語による収録に切り替わりました。同個所までの内容は英語による収録とその和訳、それ以降の内容は日本語による収録とその英訳です。

This book is the transcript of spiritual messages given by the guardian spirit of Philippines President Duterte.

These spiritual messages were channeled through Ryuho Okawa. However, please note that because of his high level of enlightenment, his way of receiving spiritual messages is fundamentally different from other psychic mediums who undergo trances and are completely taken over by the spirits they are channeling.

Each human soul is made up of six soul siblings, one of whom acts as the guardian spirit of the person living on earth. People living on earth are connected to their guardian spirits at the innermost subconscious level. They are a part of people's very souls and therefore, exact reflections of their thoughts and philosophies.

It should be noted that these spiritual messages are opinions of the individual spirits and may contradict the ideas or teachings of the Happy Science Group.

本書は、ドゥテルテ フィリピン大統領の守護霊の霊言を収録したものである。
　「霊言現象」とは、あの世の霊存在の言葉を語り下ろす現象のことをいう。これは高度な悟りを開いた者に特有のものであり、「霊媒現象」（トランス状態になって意識を失い、霊が一方的にしゃべる現象）とは異なる。
　また、人間の魂は６人のグループからなり、あの世に残っている「魂の兄弟」の１人が守護霊を務めている。つまり、守護霊は、実は自分自身の魂の一部である。
　したがって、「守護霊の霊言」とは、いわば、本人の潜在意識にアクセスしたものであり、その内容は、その人が潜在意識で考えていること（本心）と考えてよい。
　ただ、「霊言」は、あくまでも霊人の意見であり、幸福の科学グループとしての見解と矛盾する内容を含む場合がある点、付記しておきたい。

Spiritual Interview with the Guardian Spirit of the Philippines President Duterte

October 29, 2016 at Happy Science General Headquarters, Tokyo
Spiritual Interview with the Guardian Spirit of Philippines President Duterte

ドゥテルテ フィリピン大統領
守護霊メッセージ

2016年10月29日　東京都・幸福の科学総合本部にて
ドゥテルテ フィリピン大統領守護霊霊言

Rodrigo Duterte (1945~)

A Filipino politician. Born in Leyte. Upon graduating from the Lyceum of the Philippines University's Political Science Department, he passed his bar examination and became a public prosecutor. Since 1988, he served as the mayor of Davao for a total of seven terms over 22 years, improving the safety and economic conditions of the city. He took office as the 16th president of the Philippines in Jun. 2016. As a person who makes extreme remarks, he has been called the "Filipino Donald Trump." Duterte has used strong measures to crack down on narcotics and has executed one thousand several hundred suspects in several months via the police. In Oct. 2016, he visited Japan to hold a summit with Prime Minister Abe and agreed to solve the issue of the South China Sea peacefully under the rule of law. They agreed to a total and maximum yen loan of 21.4 billion yen.

Interviewers from Happy Science

Yuki Oikawa

> Director of Foreign Affairs
> Happiness Realization Party

Toshihisa Sakakibara

> Executive Director
> Director General of International El Cantare-Belief
> Promotion Division

Jiro Ayaori

> Managing Director
> Chief Editor of *The Liberty*
> Lecturer of Happy Science University

※ Interviewers are listed in the order that they appear in the transcript.
   The professional titles represent the position at the time of the interview.

ロドリゴ・ドゥテルテ（1945 －）

フィリピンの政治家。レイテ島出身。フィリピン・リセウム大学政治学部を卒業後、司法試験に合格し、検察官となる。1988 年以降、ダバオ市長を通算 7 期 22 年務め、治安や経済状況を改善した。2016 年 6 月、第 16 代大統領に就任。過激な発言を行う人物として知られ、「フィリピンのドナルド・トランプ」とも揶揄される。麻薬取り締まりに強硬な手法を持ち込み、数カ月で千数百人の麻薬犯罪容疑者が警官に殺害された。同年 10 月、来日して安倍総理と首脳会談を行い、南シナ海問題を、法の支配に基づき平和的に解決することで一致すると共に、総額約 214 億円を上限とする円借款供与で合意した。

質問者（幸福の科学）

及川幸久（幸福実現党外務局長）

榊原俊尚（幸福の科学理事　兼
　　　　　国際エル・カンターレ信仰伝道局長）

綾織次郎（幸福の科学常務理事　兼　「ザ・リバティ」
　　　　　編集長　兼　HSU 講師）

※質問順。役職は収録当時のもの。

1 Looking through the Mind of the Mysterious President Duterte

Ryuho Okawa Good afternoon, everyone. This is my first contact. So, I cannot guarantee whether we can succeed or not, he is a good man or a bad man, I don't know. His god is an evil spirit or not, I don't know. He is gentle or not, I don't know. And in addition to that, it's very difficult to understand Tagalog English*, so [*to Sakakibara*†] you, transfer Tagalog English [*audience laugh*].

Sometimes his English could be read as Chinese or Spanish or like that. But in reality, it's English, so it's very difficult for me. But I can't speak Tagalog English correctly, so please forgive me about that. But I will try my best. I have not examined what he said, his guardian spirit says, what language his guardian spirit says, so it's

---

* Tagalog and English are the official languages of the Philippines. Their English has a Tagalog accent to it.

† Sakakibara, who is one of the interviewers, has experience as a branch manager at a Happy Science branch in the Philippines.

1 「謎の人物」ドゥテルテ大統領の心を見抜く

大川隆法　みなさん、こんにちは。接触するのは今回が初めてですので、成功するかどうか保証はできません。良い人か悪い人かも分かりませんし、彼の「神」が悪霊なのかそうでないのか、親切かそうでないかも分かりません。さらには、タガログ・イングリッシュ（注1）は非常に理解しにくいので、あなた（榊原・注2）がタガログ・イングリッシュを伝達してください（会場笑）。

　彼の英語は中国語やスペイン語のようなときもありますが、実は英語なので、非常に難しいのです。私はタガログ・イングリッシュは正確には話せませんので、それについてはご容赦ください。ただ、ベストは尽くします。彼が何を言ったか、彼の守護霊が何を言うか、守護霊が何語を話すのかも調べておりませんので、英語か日本語か、それ

（注1）フィリピンの公用語はタガログ語と英語だが、英語にはタガログ語のなまりがある。
（注2）質問者の一人である榊原は、フィリピンにある幸福の科学の支部で支部長を務めた経験がある。

English or Japanese or another language, I don't know.

So, in reality, this is the first contact. But I think he is very mysterious and just one or two days ago, he left Japan. We know only about the fact that he had a conversation with Xi Jinping in China and in Tokyo, Mr. Abe or other people*. And we are much troubled with his different opinion about China or the United States. So, today's main aim is, "What kind of a person is he?" No one knows correctly. Of course, Philippine people know a lot about him, but we, Japanese, cannot understand him correctly. And of course, people in the United States don't know him well.

1 「謎の人物」ドゥテルテ大統領の心を見抜く

以外の言語を話すのかも分かりません。

　実際、今回が最初のコンタクトですが、非常に謎めいた人物だと思います。ちょうど一日、二日前に日本を発ったところで、中国で習近平氏と会談し、日本では安倍さんや他の方と会談したという事実しか分かっていません（注）。中国やアメリカに関するこの人の意見は変わっていて、かなり翻弄されておりますので、今日の主たる目的は、「この人は、いかなる人物であるのか」ということです。誰も正確なところは知りません。もちろん、フィリピンの人たちは彼をよく知っているのでしょうが、私たち日本人は正確には分かりませんし、もちろんアメリカの人たちもよく知りません。

（注）ドゥテルテ大統領は2016年10月20日、中国国家主席の習近平氏と北京で会談し、約2.5兆円の経済協力の約束を取り付ける一方、中国が領有権を主張している南シナ海問題では、事実上棚上げの姿勢を示した。その後一度帰国した後に訪日。10月26日に安倍首相と会談し（左写真）、日本の大型巡視船2隻の供与、50億円の円借款の実施等で合意した。南シナ海問題についてドゥテルテ大統領は、「日本とわが国は同じ状況にあると考えている」「常に日本の側に立つつもりだ」と発言した。

★ President Duterte had talks with Chinese President Xi Jinping in Beijing on Oct. 20, 2016. While agreeing to a promise of approximately 2.5 trillion yen in economic cooperation, he shelved the issue of Chinese sovereignty over the South China Sea. Duterte then returned home before visiting Japan. He and Prime Minister Abe met (left photo) and agreed on the supplying of two Japanese large-scale patrol boats and five billion yen loan, among other things, on Oct. 26. In regards to the issue of the South China Sea, President Duterte claimed that he thinks of the situation as similar to Japan's and that he intends to always stand by Japan.

But we have some kind of impression that he can be some kind of troublesome figure in the Asian district. So, is he a friend of China or a friend of Japan or a friend of the United States? Or, is he just thinking about his country only? We must look through his mind and make up our plan on how to deal with or cooperate with Philippine people or country or this president.

It's up to you, so I rely on you. But if some accident happens, at that time, please change your mind and settle the battle or some misleading conversation. I hope so. If it's difficult for you to speak in Tagalog English, you can use Japanese. I can understand and I will transfer the contents to him. He will say some kind of language at that time. OK, then, we'll try.

We will invite Mr. Rodrigo Duterte, the guardian spirit of Mr. President of the Philippines, Mr. Duterte, the guardian spirit of Mr. Duterte, would you come down here and answer our questions? Mr. Duterte, the guardian spirit of Mr. Du…

ただ、この人はアジア地域における一種の「問題児」になることは有り得るという印象は受けますので、彼は中国の友人なのか日本の友人か、あるいはアメリカの友人なのか、もしくは単に自分の国のことしか考えていないのか、その心を見抜かなければなりません。そして、フィリピンの人たち、フィリピンという国、この大統領にどう対処していくか、あるいは協力していくか、計画を練らなければいけません。

（質問者の）あなたがたにかかっていますので、あなたがたが頼りですけれども、もし何かアクシデントが起きた場合は考え方を変えて、論争や誤解を招くやり取りをうまく収めていただければと思います。タガログ・イングリッシュで話すことが難しいようであれば、日本語を使ってかまいません。私が理解できますので、内容を彼に伝えます。そうすれば、何語かで話してくれるでしょう。よろしいですか。では、やってみましょう。

　ロドリゴ・ドゥテルテ氏、フィリピン大統領の守護霊をお招きいたします。ドゥテルテ氏よ、ドゥテルテ氏の守護霊よ、どうかここに降りたまいて、私たちの質問にお答えください。ドゥテルテ氏よ、ドゥテルテ氏の守護霊よ……。

2 Impression of the Visit to Japan and of Prime Minister Abe

The guardian spirit somehow knows about Japanese Shinto

Duterte's Guardian Spirit Uhn. Ahhhh. A-ha, ha.

Yuki Oikawa Mr. President. [*Duterte's G.S. suddenly gets out of his chair and takes off his suit.*] [*Audience laugh.*] Hello? Hello, Mr. President? Hello. Let me confirm. Are you the guardian spirit of President Duterte?

Duterte's G.S. What is a guardian spirit? Uh?

Oikawa OK. So, you are President Duterte?

Duterte's G.S. Duterte, Duterte, ah, yeah.

2　訪日の感想と安倍首相の印象は？

なぜか日本神道の知識があるドゥテルテ守護霊

ドゥテルテ守護霊　うー、あー……アハ、ハア。

及川幸久　大統領……（ドゥテルテ氏の守護霊、突如、椅子から立ち上がり、背広の上着を脱ぎ捨てる）（会場笑）ハロー？　ハロー、大統領？　ハロー。確認させていただきますが、ドゥテルテ大統領の守護霊でいらっしゃいますか。

ドゥテルテ守護霊　「守護霊」って何だよ。

及川　では、ドゥテルテ大統領でいらっしゃいますか。

ドゥテルテ守護霊　そう、ドゥテルテ、ドゥテルテだよ。

2 Impression of the Visit to Japan and of Prime Minister Abe

Oikawa OK. OK, yeah. It's a big honor having this session today here with you.

Duterte's G.S. *Owner?* Owner? What's owner?

Oikawa It's our pleasure. It's our big…

Duterte's G.S. Ah, *honor.* Uh? Honor, honor, honor, honor, honor, honor, OK.

Oikawa Thank you very much for coming today. And especially…

Duterte's G.S. Who are you? Who are you?

Oikawa We are Happy Science.

Duterte's G.S. What's that?

及川　はい、分かりました。本日はこのような機会をいただき、たいへん光栄（honorオナー）です。

ドゥテルテ守護霊　オーナー（owner 所有者）？　オーナー？　オーナーって何が？

及川　たいへん、うれしく思っています。非常に……。

ドゥテルテ守護霊　ああ、「光栄」？　光栄、光栄ね、オーケー。

及川　本日はお越しいただきまことにありがとうございます。特に……。

ドゥテルテ守護霊　君たち誰なの？　誰？

及川　私たちはハッピー・サイエンスです。

ドゥテルテ守護霊　何それ？

Oikawa We are Happy Science.

Duterte's G.S. What's that?

Oikawa The biggest Japanese spiritual group.

Duterte's G.S. Really? Really?

Oikawa Yes.

Duterte's G.S. No, no. *Ise-jingu* is the greatest.

Oikawa You are talking about Shintoism, right?

Duterte's G.S. Bigger. Bigger.

Toshihisa Sakakibara Japanese Shintoism. Yeah, we are different.

Duterte's G.S. Different?

及川　ハッピー・サイエンスです。

ドゥテルテ守護霊　何それ？

及川　日本最大の宗教団体です。

ドゥテルテ守護霊　本当、本当に？

及川　はい。

ドゥテルテ守護霊　違う違う。伊勢神宮(いせじんぐう)が最大だろう。

及川　神道のことをおっしゃっているんですね。

ドゥテルテ守護霊　もっと大きいだろう。もっと。

榊原俊尚　日本神道はですね、はい。私たちは違います。

ドゥテルテ守護霊　違う？

Sakakibara Yeah, a new religion in Japan.

Duterte's G.S. [*Looking at Sakakibara.*] Oh, you are Filipino.

[*Audience laugh.*]

Sakakibara Yeah, I almost look like a Filipino, but I'm actually Japanese.

Duterte's G.S. Really? Oh.

Sakakibara But I used to live in the Philippines for two years. So, I'm very familiar with the Philippines. I'm very happy to see you, finally.

Duterte's G.S. Really? Uh, I think so.

Sakakibara Yes.

榊原　はい、日本の新しい宗教です。

ドゥテルテ守護霊　（榊原を見て）ああ、君はフィリピン人か。

（会場笑）

榊原　はい、ほとんどフィリピン人に見えますが、実際は日本人です。

ドゥテルテ守護霊　本当？　へえ。

榊原　ただ、フィリピンには２年間住んでいましたので、フィリピンにはたいへん、なじみがあります。ですので、ようやくお会いすることができ、たいへん、うれしく思っております。

ドゥテルテ守護霊　本当？　ふうん、こちらこそ。

榊原　はい。

2 Impression of the Visit to Japan and of Prime Minister Abe

Feeling very sorry about missing the meeting with the "god emperor" of Japan

Oikawa Thank you, thank you for coming. So, first of all, you've just been to Japan and I know you have been here before to Japan, but this time it's official, right?

Duterte's G.S. Ah, you, speak slowly. Your English is not correct. OK?

Oikawa OK. I will speak slowly.

Duterte's G.S. Slowly. Correctly.

Oikawa OK. You have been to Japan, right?

Duterte's G.S. Yeah.

「神」としての天皇陛下に会えず残念がる

及川　お越しくださり、まことにありがとうございます。それでは、まず初めに、ちょうどあなたは来日されていました。以前も日本に来られたことがあったと思いますが、今回は公式訪問でしたね。

ドゥテルテ守護霊　ああ、君、もっとゆっくり話しなさいよ。君の英語はおかしいよ。分かる？

及川　分かりました。ゆっくり話します。

ドゥテルテ守護霊　ゆっくり、正しく。

及川　はい。来日されていましたね。

ドゥテルテ守護霊　ああ。

2 Impression of the Visit to Japan and of Prime Minister Abe

Oikawa Then, what was your impression of your visit this week?

Duterte's G.S. Uhn, uhn, I wanted to meet emperor, emperor, god emperor.

Oikawa Sorry for the cancellation of that session.

Duterte's G.S. Very sorry. I kill someone.

Sakakibara How did you feel about that? So, you missed…

Duterte's G.S. About that?

Sakakibara Yeah. You missed the opportunity to meet the emperor of Japan.

Duterte's G.S. Hmm… It means the emperor of Japan was very afraid of meeting with me because I am

2 訪日の感想と安倍首相の印象は？

及川　今週、訪日された際の印象は、いかがでしたでしょうか。

ドゥテルテ守護霊　うーん。天皇陛下にお会いしたかったね。現人神（あらひとがみ）たる陛下に。

及川　謁見（えっけん）がキャンセルになって残念でした。

ドゥテルテ守護霊　実に残念だ。誰か殺してやるかな。

榊原　それについて、どうお感じでしたか。あいにく……。

ドゥテルテ守護霊　そのことをか？

榊原　はい。天皇陛下にお会いする機会を逃（のが）されて。

ドゥテルテ守護霊　うーん……。私がフィリピンの〝最高神〟だから、天皇陛下は私と会うのがすごく怖かったんだ

the greatest god of the Philippines, so that's the reason.

The one word to describe Prime Minister Abe

Oikawa OK, what was your impression meeting with Mr. Abe?

Duterte's G.S. Abe.

Oikawa Mr. Abe.

Duterte's G.S. Abe. *Kechi* (Stingy) Abe.

Oikawa [*Laughs.*]

[*Audience laugh.*]

Duterte's G.S. Kechi Abe, kechi Abe, kechi Abe. Abe, Abe kechi, haha. Kechi, you know?

ろう。そういうわけよ。

安倍首相の印象は「一言(ひとこと)」に尽きる

及川　分かりました。では、安倍さんに会った印象はいかがでしたか。

ドゥテルテ守護霊　安倍ね。

及川　安倍さんです。

ドゥテルテ守護霊　安倍。「ケチ安倍」。

及川　（笑）

（会場笑）

ドゥテルテ守護霊　ケチ安倍、ケチ安倍、ケチ安倍。安倍。安倍はケチ。ハハ。ケチって分かるだろう。

Jiro Ayaori Do you want…

Duterte's G.S. *Kechi* is English, ah, you know?

Oikawa No.

Duterte's G.S. Oh…

Ayaori Do you want more support from Japan?

Duterte's G.S. Ah… You know the amount China gave me, you know?

Ayaori Yes.

Duterte's G.S. Hmm… Two, hmm… two thousand five hundred billion yen they gave me?

Ayaori Hmm…

綾織次郎　あなたは……。

ドゥテルテ守護霊　「ケチ」は英語だよな。

及川　いえ。

ドゥテルテ守護霊　ああ……。

綾織　日本からもっと援助してほしいわけですか。

ドゥテルテ守護霊　ああ。中国がくれた金額、知ってるか。

綾織　はい。

ドゥテルテ守護霊　えーと……２兆５千億円くれたんだぞ。

綾織　ええ。

2 Impression of the Visit to Japan and of Prime Minister Abe

Duterte's G.S. Japan, five billion yen*? Hmm? What is… huh, huh? Explain to me…

Oikawa So, you expected more money from Japan, right?

Duterte's G.S. Of course, of course. Japan should com… Oh, more competition, need more competition with China and must win China.

Sakakibara That's your real intention toward China, right?

Duterte's G.S. Hmm… Kechi, Abe kechi, kechi Abe, Abe kechi, Abe…

Sakakibara We'll talk to him.

---

* The yen loan is approximately five billion yen in funds but, in addition, Japan will construct two large-scale patrol vessels and deliver them to the Philippines after completion. Japan will offer approximately 16.4 billion yen in loans as construction cost.

ドゥテルテ守護霊　日本は50億円（注）だろ。何だよ。説明してよ。

及川　では、日本にもっと大きな金額を期待しておられたんですね。

ドゥテルテ守護霊　当たり前だろう。日本はもっと競争しなきゃ駄目だ。もっと中国と競争して、中国に勝たなきゃいかんだろう。

榊原　中国に対して、本心ではそう思っていらっしゃるんですね。

ドゥテルテ守護霊　うーん。ケチだ。安倍ケチ。ケチ安倍。安倍ケチ。安倍は……。

榊原　彼に話しておきます。

（注）資金の形での円借款は約50億円だが、加えて大型巡視船を日本で２隻建造し、完成後フィリピンに引き渡す。建造費の約164億円も円借款で提供する。

Duterte's G.S. Abe kechi *de*, Abe kechi. Uncle of emperor of Japan die* because of kechi Abe.

Sakakibara [*Laughs.*] I see. OK.

Oikawa OK. We're asking you about China later…

Duterte's G.S. I…slowly, slowly.

Oikawa [*Laughs.*] Slowly, OK.

Duterte's G.S. Correct English is very slow.

Oikawa All right, all right.

Duterte's G.S. You know?

---

* On Oct. 27, 2016, His Imperial Highness Prince Takahito Mikasanomiya, uncle to the current emperor, had passed away due to heart failure.

ドゥテルテ守護霊　安倍ケチで、安倍ケチ。ケチ安倍のせいで天皇陛下の叔父さんが亡くなったんだ。(注)

榊原　(笑)なるほど、分かりました。

及川　はい。中国については、また後ほど伺います。

ドゥテルテ守護霊　だから、もっとゆっくりだって。

及川　(笑)ゆっくりですね、はい。

ドゥテルテ守護霊　正しい英語は、すごくゆっくりなんだから。

及川　はい、大丈夫です。

ドゥテルテ守護霊　分かるかな。

(注) 2016年10月27日、今上天皇の叔父にあたる三笠宮崇仁親王が、心不全で薨去（こうきょ）された。

3 "Just Kill Bad People"

The "open secret" of his success as mayor

Oikawa So, your hometown is Davao in Mindanao, and you are the former mayor of Davao, right?

Duterte's G.S. Mayor, hmm...

Oikawa And during your time, Davao changed and became very prosperous, and became...

Duterte's G.S. Prosper...

Oikawa Yeah. And became...

Duterte's G.S. Good. Good, good. Sounds good.

Oikawa And very safe.

3 「悪い奴らを殺すだけ」

市長時代に成功した理由は「公然の秘密」

及川　あなたの故郷はミンダナオ島のダバオで、ダバオの前市長でいらっしゃいますね。

ドゥテルテ守護霊　市長、うん。

及川　あなたの任期中にダバオは変わり、非常に繁栄しました。

ドゥテルテ守護霊　繁栄だよ。

及川　はい。そして……。

ドゥテルテ守護霊　いいねいいね、いいね。いい響きだ。

及川　非常に治安(ちあん)が良くなりました。

3 "Just Kill Bad People"

Duterte's G.S. Safe… Hmm…

Oikawa Right? So, I think…

Duterte's G.S. Safe, safer, safest.

Oikawa Yes. I think you are very good at doing economic policies. So, what was your secret?

Duterte's G.S. Secret? Just kill bad people*.

[*Audience laugh.*]

Duterte's G.S. That's the secret. Not a secret. It's an open secret.

---

* Since President Duterte's assumption in office, he has been cracking down on drug crimes and has accepted "extra-legal murders" in which the police and neighborhood watchers execute suspects without trial. It is said that there have been over 2,000 suspects executed in this drug war, but his approval ratings from the citizens remain high.

3 「悪い奴らを殺すだけ」

ドゥテルテ守護霊　治安ね。うーん。

及川　でしたよね。ですから……。

ドゥテルテ守護霊　治安よし、治安向上、治安最高。

及川　はい。経済政策がたいへん得意でいらっしゃると思うのですが、その秘密は何だったのでしょうか。

ドゥテルテ守護霊　秘密って、悪い奴らを殺すだけだから。(注)

(会場笑)

ドゥテルテ守護霊　それが秘密だ。秘密じゃないな。公然(こうぜん)の秘密だ。

（注）ドゥテルテ大統領は就任以来、麻薬犯罪の取り締まり強化を進め、警官や自警団が裁判なしで容疑者を殺害する「超法規的殺人」を容認している。この「麻薬戦争」で殺害された容疑者は2000人以上と言われるが、ドゥテルテ氏は国民からの高い支持率を維持している。

Oikawa [*Laughs.*] Open secret.

"You need to pull off the bad tooth"

Sakakibara Yeah. Your way is kind of extreme.

Duterte's G.S. Oh… Your Tagalog English is not so correct.

[*Audience laugh.*]

Sakakibara [*Laughs.*] I'm very sorry. Your way to kill people to make peace is kind of extreme.

Duterte's G.S. Huh?

Sakakibara Extreme. But…

Duterte's G.S. Are you speaking English?

3 「悪い奴らを殺すだけ」

及川　（笑）公然の秘密ですか。

「悪い歯は抜かないと駄目」

榊原　そうですね。あなたのやり方は、いささか極端です。

ドゥテルテ守護霊　ああ、君のタガログ・イングリッシュは、あまり正しくない。

（会場笑）

榊原　（笑）申し訳ありません。平和をもたらすために人を殺すというやり方は、やや極端です。

ドゥテルテ守護霊　うん？

榊原　極端ではありますが……。

ドゥテルテ守護霊　君、英語を話してるの？

3 "Just Kill Bad People"

Sakakibara [*Laughs.*] Yeah.

Duterte's G.S. Really?

Sakakibara [*Laughs.*] Sorry.

Duterte's G.S. Uh-huh.

Sakakibara People in the Philippines are very happy, especially in Davao.

Duterte's G.S. Uh-huh.

Sakakibara And I heard about you a lot that you were a very good mayor in Davao, and improved a lot of things. So…

Duterte's G.S. Good is not enough.

Sakakibara Excellent.

榊原　（笑）はい。

ドゥテルテ守護霊　本当かねえ。

榊原　（笑）申し訳ありません。

ドゥテルテ守護霊　ああ。

榊原　フィリピンの人たち、特にダバオの人たちは非常に幸福です。

ドゥテルテ守護霊　ああ。

榊原　ダバオでは非常にいい市長でいらして、いろいろ改善されたという話を、よくお聞きしました。ですから……。

ドゥテルテ守護霊　「いい」という言葉じゃあ足らんね。

榊原　「優秀な。」

3 "Just Kill Bad People"

Duterte's G.S. Capable or excellent.

Sakakibara Most excellent mayor in the Philippines.

Duterte's G.S. Yeah. Most talented.

Sakakibara So, we'd like to know about you more because you are a kind of a mysterious person for us...

Duterte's G.S. Uh-huh.

Sakakibara ...For the people not only in Japan, but also in the world. So, could you tell us about your basic philosophy or belief? How you...

Duterte's G.S. Basic philosophy?

Sakakibara Yes. How you founded the way to...

Duterte's G.S. Where are you from? From Greek?

3 「悪い奴らを殺すだけ」

ドゥテルテ守護霊　「有能な」とか「優秀な」とか。

榊原　フィリピン一、優秀な市長でした。

ドゥテルテ守護霊　そう。「最も才能溢れた」。

榊原　ですから、もっとあなたについて知りたく思います。私たちにとって、ある意味、謎めいた方ですので。

ドゥテルテ守護霊　ああ。

榊原　日本人だけでなく、世界中の人たちにとってです。そこで、あなたの基本哲学あるいは信条について教えていただけますでしょうか。どうやって……。

ドゥテルテ守護霊　基本哲学？

榊原　はい。どのように……。

ドゥテルテ守護霊　君、どこの人？　ギリシャ？

Sakakibara Ah, me?

Duterte's G.S. Uh.

[*Audience laugh.*]

Sakakibara I'm Japanese.

Duterte's G.S. Oh… Japanese, OK. Philosophy?

Sakakibara Philosophy or belief in yourself.

Duterte's G.S. Kill people. Bad people.

Sakakibara [*Laughs.*] So, how did you reach that way of thinking in order to make peace or bring peace? Why did you reach that kind of belief to bring peace, to kill the people is the best way?

Duterte's G.S. Umm. When your tooth hurts, you

榊原　私ですか。

ドゥテルテ守護霊　うん。

(会場笑)

榊原　日本人ですが。

ドゥテルテ守護霊　ああ、日本人。そう。哲学？

榊原　ご自身の「哲学」や「信条」です。

ドゥテルテ守護霊　殺せ。悪人は殺せ。

榊原　(笑)では、平和をもたらすために、どのようにして、そう考えるに至ったのでしょうか。なぜ、「平和をもたらすには人を殺すことが一番である」と考えるに至ったのですか。

ドゥテルテ守護霊　うーん、歯が痛い時はペンチが必要で、

need a *penchi* (pliers) and pull off the bad tooth. It's the only way to solve your…

Same answer when asked about the future vision of the Philippines

Ayaori So, what is your vision of the future Philippines?

Duterte's G.S. *Pigeon*? Pigeon? Pigeon is good for French (cuisine)…

Ayaori French?

Duterte's G.S. French? Pigeon, pigeon. You like pigeon?

Ayaori No, sorry.

Duterte's G.S. No?

3　「悪い奴らを殺すだけ」

悪い歯は抜かないと駄目だ。問題を解決するにはそれしか……。

「フィリピンの未来ビジョン」を聞かれても一貫した答え

綾織　では、どのようなフィリピンの未来ビジョンをお持ちですか。

ドゥテルテ守護霊　鳩(はと)（pigeon ピジョン）？　鳩？　鳩はフランス料理に向いてるけど。

綾織　フレンチ？

ドゥテルテ守護霊　フレンチ？　鳩、鳩。君は鳩が好きなわけ？

綾織　いえ、すみません。

ドゥテルテ守護霊　違うの？

3 "Just Kill Bad People"

Ayaori Your *vision*.

Duterte's G.S. Vision?

Ayaori Future Philippines…

Duterte's G.S. Vision…vision…vision…

Oikawa Future. Your future image of your country.

Duterte's G.S. To kill bad people completely. Last one or he come to police or kill the last one. Like *Gokiburi* (cockroach). No? Ban, ban, ban!

Oikawa OK, you mean bad people are maybe doing drugs…

Duterte's G.S. And I'm the Batman of Philippines.

綾織　あなたの「ビジョン」です。

ドゥテルテ守護霊　ビジョン？

綾織　フィリピンの未来に……。

ドゥテルテ守護霊　ビジョン、ビジョン、ビジョン……。

及川　未来です。あなたの国の未来のイメージです。

ドゥテルテ守護霊　悪人は徹底的に殺す。最後の一人が警察に来たら、そいつを殺す。ゴキブリみたいに。違うか？　バン、バン、バン！

及川　はい、悪人とは、おそらく麻薬……。

ドゥテルテ守護霊　私はフィリピンのバットマンだから。

Oikawa Batman. OK. So, I think you are targeting the drug addicts.

Duterte's G.S. We have four million people.

Oikawa Drug addicts?

Duterte's G.S. Yeah, yeah, yeah.

Oikawa Right. So, you are going to…

Duterte's G.S. I must kill all of them but if they convert their hearts to God, I will give them forgiveness.

Oikawa Yes, but drug business is dominated by China. So, your country receives so many drugs from China. So, if you really solve this problem…

Duterte's G.S. And people of our country sell drugs to Japan, Japanese people, Japanese Yakuza. So, I am

及川　バットマン。なるほど。麻薬中毒者をターゲットにされているのだと思います。

ドゥテルテ守護霊　400万人いるからね。

及川　麻薬中毒者が？

ドゥテルテ守護霊　そう、そう、そう。

及川　そうですね。ですから、あなたは……。

ドゥテルテ守護霊　そいつら全員、殺さなければいかんのだが、神に向けて回心(かいしん)するなら許してやる。

及川　はい、しかし、麻薬ビジネスは中国に支配されています。あなたの国には中国から大量に麻薬が入ってきていますので、この問題を本気で解決したければ……。

ドゥテルテ守護霊　フィリピン人は麻薬を日本人に、日本のやくざに売ってるんで、私は実のところ、日本のために

working for Japan in reality.

Oikawa You're going to fight against China's drug industry?

Duterte's G.S. China's drug? Your English is very difficult. China's drug? Fight with China's drug? China's yakuza? China's drug? China's bad people? Criminal?

Oikawa I mean China is sending many drugs to the Philippines.

Duterte's G.S. No, no, no, no, no. We are producing drugs in our country. China is an importer from us.

働いてるんだよ。

及川　中国の麻薬産業と戦うおつもりですか。

ドゥテルテ守護霊　中国麻薬？　君の英語は、えらく難しいな。中国麻薬？　中国麻薬と戦う？　中国やくざ？　中国麻薬？　中国の悪人？　犯罪人？

及川　中国がフィリピンに麻薬を大量に送り込んでいるということです。

ドゥテルテ守護霊　違う、違う、違う、違う。麻薬は国内で生産してるんだよ。中国は、うちから輸入してるんで。

4 How Does He See America and Japan as the God of the Philippines?

Officially a Catholic, but who is his God?

Sakakibara May I ask your religious belief?

Duterte's G.S. Religious belief?

Sakakibara Because you have that kind of a belief…

Duterte's G.S. I am a person of mercy.

Sakakibara Mercy? OK. Where does that thought come from?

Duterte's G.S. Come from?

4 「フィリピンの神」として
　　アメリカと日本をどう見るか

公式にはカトリック教徒だが、
実際に信じている神は誰か

榊原　あなたの宗教的信条についてお尋ねしてよろしいでしょうか。

ドゥテルテ守護霊　宗教的信条？

榊原　あなたはその種の信条……。

ドゥテルテ守護霊　私は「慈悲深き人」ですよ。

榊原　慈悲ですか。分かりました。そのお考えはどこから来ているのでしょうか。

ドゥテルテ守護霊　どこからって？

Sakakibara Yes. I heard the rumor that you are a Muslim believer. No? Or a Christian?

Duterte's G.S. Maybe I am a… I am the god of Philippines, so is this Muslim or Catholic, I don't know. But I am a god. I'm a god.

Oikawa Officially, you are Catholic.

Duterte's G.S. Officially, yes.

Oikawa But maybe not. Are you Muslim?

Duterte's G.S. No.

Oikawa Who is your God?

Duterte's G.S. My God? Oh, I am God.

榊原　はい。イスラム教徒でいらっしゃるという噂を聞きました。違いますか。それともキリスト教徒ですか。

ドゥテルテ守護霊　たぶん……私は〝フィリピンの神〟だから、イスラム教徒かカトリックかは知らん。だが、私は〝神〟だよ。〝神様〟だから。

及川　公式にはカトリックでいらっしゃいます。

ドゥテルテ守護霊　公式には、そうだ。

及川　ただ、違うかもしれません。イスラム教徒なのですか。

ドゥテルテ守護霊　違う。

及川　あなたの神はどなたですか。

ドゥテルテ守護霊　私の神？　ああ、私が神だよ。

4 How Does He See America and Japan as the God of the Philippines?

Oikawa You are? You are God?

Duterte's G.S. Yes.

The truth about the voice of God he heard on the airplane

Sakakibara But recently when you arrived to Davao City and you had an interview with the reporters, you answered…

Duterte's G.S. Reporter. Reporter, reporter… pronounce correctly. *Reporter.* OK?

Sakakibara Sorry, my poor pronunciation. But, so your answer to the reporters was that you heard God's calling*. Ah, the God's calling that…

---

* Upon his return from Japan on Oct. 27, President Duterte held a press conference to announce that he would refrain from using harsh language, the reason being that he had received a calling from God.

4 「フィリピンの神」としてアメリカと日本をどう見るか

及川 あなたが? あなたが神なのですか。

ドゥテルテ守護霊 そうです。

「飛行機で聞いた神の声」の真相は?

榊原 ただ、最近ダバオ市に着いた時、リポーターからインタビューを受けてお答えになったのは……。

ドゥテルテ守護霊 リポーター、リポーター、リポーター。発音は正しく。「リポーター」だよ。分かる?

榊原 発音が下手で申し訳ありません。ただ、リポーターたちへのお答えでは、「神のお告げ」を聞かれたと(注)。その「神のお告げ」とは……。

(注)ドゥテルテ大統領は日本から帰国した10月27日、会見を開き、「神のお告げがあった」という理由で、これまで繰り返していた暴言をやめると宣言した。

Duterte's G.S. God is meaning me.

Sakakibara You, yourself?

Duterte's G.S. Me, me. Yeah.

Sakakibara But you said, superficially, that you have received the message from God. And then, the God said that if you continue to speak ill of others very badly, He would let the airplane go down. So, what is the meaning of that message or who is the God you are talking to?

Duterte's G.S. Almighty God.

Sakakibara Almighty God? OK.

Duterte's G.S. I swear I'll never say Mr. Barack Obama is a son of prostitute before I kill him.

ドゥテルテ守護霊 「神」とは私のことだから。

榊原 あなたご自身ですか。

ドゥテルテ守護霊 私ですよ、私。ええ。

榊原 ただ、言葉としては、「神のお告げがあった」と言われました。その神は、「お前が人に対して暴言を吐き続けるなら、この飛行機を墜落させる」とおっしゃったと。そのメッセージの意味するところは何だったのでしょうか。あなたが話された「神」とは誰なのでしょうか。

ドゥテルテ守護霊 全能の神だよ。

榊原 全能の神ですか。なるほど。

ドゥテルテ守護霊 「バラク・オバマ氏は売春婦の息子だ」などとは決して言わないと誓った。彼を殺す前に。

Sakakibara [*Laughs.*] Before you…

Ayaori So, did you send that message to Mr. Duterte?

Duterte's G.S. Huh?

Ayaori In the prayer?

Duterte's G.S. Yeah, we are one.

Ayaori Did you say that?

Duterte's G.S. I'm a god and he's god's son.

Sakakibara Actually, Mr. Duterte received the message from the guardian spirit of himself. OK? That's the meaning.

4 「フィリピンの神」としてアメリカと日本をどう見るか

榊原　（笑）彼を……。

綾織　では、あなたがドゥテルテ氏にそのメッセージを送られたのでしょうか。

ドゥテルテ守護霊　うん？

綾織　祈りの中で？

ドゥテルテ守護霊　そう、われわれは一体だから。

綾織　あなたが、そうおっしゃったのでしょうか。

ドゥテルテ守護霊　私は〝神〟で、彼は〝神の息子〟だから。

榊原　実際には、「ドゥテルテ氏は自分の守護霊のメッセージを受け取った」ということでよろしいでしょうか。そういう意味だと。

4 How Does He See America and Japan as the God of the Philippines?

Duterte's G.S. Yeah. He is the only son of god. The god is me. OK?

Sakakibara OK. OK.

His connection to Typhoon Haiyan that attacked the Philippines

Oikawa OK. OK. You talked about the god of the Philippines.

Duterte's G.S. Yeah.

Oikawa And in the past, 2013, we had a big typhoon which was called Haiyan.

Duterte's G.S. Oh, Haiyan.

Oikawa That time, we had this kind of spiritual interview right here and we realized…*

ドゥテルテ守護霊　ああ。彼（地上のドゥテルテ大統領）は〝神の独り子〟で、「神」は〝私〟（守護霊）です。いいかな。

榊原　はい、分かりました。

フィリピンを襲った台風ハイエンとの関係

及川　はい、分かりました。「フィリピンの神」とおっしゃいましたが。

ドゥテルテ守護霊　ああ。

及川　過去、2013年には「ハイエン」と呼ばれた大きな台風がありました。

ドゥテルテ守護霊　ああ、「ハイエン」ね。

及川　当時、ここで、こうした霊言が行われて、分かったことは……。（注）

4 How Does He See America and Japan as the God of the Philippines?

Duterte's G.S. Haiyan is my friend.

Oikawa Oh.

Duterte's G.S. He killed a lot of people instead of me killing people with gun.

Oikawa Haiyan said that Haiyan is the sea god of Philippines. So, he…

Duterte's G.S. Sea god? Then I'm the god of Heaven.

Oikawa God of Heaven?

ドゥテルテ守護霊　ハイエンとは友だちだよ。

及川　おお。

ドゥテルテ守護霊　私が銃で人を殺す代わりに、あちらが大勢、殺したわけだ。

及川　ハイエンは、「自分はフィリピンの海神(かいじん)だ」と言っていました。では彼は……。

ドゥテルテ守護霊　海神？　なら、私は「天の神」です。

及川　「天の神」ですか。

（注）2013年11月12日、大川隆法総裁は、フィリピンを襲った巨大台風「ハイエン」の霊査を行った。台風の霊的な原因をつくった霊は、「フィリピンの神」を名乗った。『フィリピン巨大台風の霊的真相を探る』（幸福の科学出版刊）参照。

★ On Nov. 12, 2013, Master Ryuho Okawa conducted a spiritual reading of Typhoon Haiyan that swept the Philippines. The spirit behind the spiritual cause of the typhoon identified itself as the god of the Philippines. See *Exploring the Spiritual Truth of the Massive Typhoon in the Philippines* (Tokyo: Happy Science, 2014).

Duterte's G.S. Yeah.

Sakakibara Of the Philippines?

Oikawa I see. So, you know Haiyan very well?

Duterte's G.S. He or she, I don't know… It is a god of the Philippines Sea, around there. And I'm shining all over the world through Heaven, meaning sky.

Oikawa I see. That time, Haiyan insisted that the U.S. troops in the Philippines should leave the Philippines. And this time, you said the same thing.

Duterte's G.S. Yeah, it's true, it's true.

Oikawa So, you really want the U.S. troops to withdraw from the Philippines?

4 「フィリピンの神」としてアメリカと日本をどう見るか

ドゥテルテ守護霊　そう。

榊原　フィリピンの、ということでしょうか。

及川　分かりました。では、ハイエンのことは、よくご存じなんですね。

ドゥテルテ守護霊　彼だか彼女だか知らんが、あれはフィリピンあたりの海神だよ。そして私は天から、空から、全世界を照らしておる。

及川　なるほど。その時ハイエンは、「フィリピンにいるアメリカ軍はフィリピンから去るべきだ」と主張していました。そして今回、あなたも同じことをおっしゃっています。

ドゥテルテ守護霊　ああ、その通り、その通り。

及川　では、本気で米軍にフィリピンから撤退してほしいのですか。

Duterte's G.S. They are intruders, so they need punishment from us. We are intruded by them. Japan, also. So, we are friends, Japan and…

Oikawa Ah, you mean, Japan and the Philippines are friends?

Duterte's G.S. Yeah, friends. We are intruded by bad America, so we are friends.

Oikawa Why America has to have punishment?

Duterte's G.S. Because they killed a lot of Philippine people. Tens of thousands of people.

Oikawa So, you are…

Duterte's G.S. Especially in Davao, around Davao, Mindanao.

4 「フィリピンの神」としてアメリカと日本をどう見るか

ドゥテルテ守護霊　奴らは侵略者だから、われわれから罰を受ける必要がある。彼らに侵略されたんで。日本もそうだ。だから、われわれは仲間なんだよ。日本と……。

及川　ああ、つまり、日本とフィリピンは仲間であると？

ドゥテルテ守護霊　ああ、仲間だよ。お互い、悪いアメリカに侵略されたわけだから、仲間だ。

及川　なぜ、アメリカは罰を受ける必要があるのでしょうか。

ドゥテルテ守護霊　フィリピン人を大勢、殺したからだよ。何万人も。

及川　では、あなたは……。

ドゥテルテ守護霊　特にダバオでね。ミンダナオ島のダバオあたりで。

83

"Japan had to kill MacArthur at that time"

Oikawa So, you are anti-white?

Duterte's G.S. White?

Oikawa White people.

Duterte's G.S. White people?

Oikawa The U.S. and western…

Duterte's G.S. You mean, stupid people? White in the brain?

Oikawa OK. From this perspective, if you look at the past history like World War II, which happened in Asian countries including the Philippines, was especially the hot place that many people died.

4 「フィリピンの神」としてアメリカと日本をどう見るか

「日本はあの時点でマッカーサーを殺すべきだった」

及川　では、あなたは「アンチ白人」なのですか。

ドゥテルテ守護霊　白？

及川　白人です。

ドゥテルテ守護霊　白人？

及川　アメリカや西洋の……。

ドゥテルテ守護霊　つまり、バカどもか？　頭の中が真っ白な？

及川　はい。この観点から過去の歴史、つまりフィリピンを含むアジア諸国で起きた第二次世界大戦を見ると、フィリピンは、特に多くの人が亡くなった戦場でした。

4 How Does He See America and Japan as the God of the Philippines?

Duterte's G.S. Uh-huh.

Oikawa So, how do you see World War II? What is your opinion?

Duterte's G.S. Oh… Japan's victory is a great one. Japan nearly escaped with the victory. Japanese army had to kill General MacArthur* at that time. That's the point.

Oikawa I see. Yeah, we really agree. So, we believe that the war was an Asian independent revolution from the White countries. Do you agree?

Duterte's G.S. Hmm… We were occupied by the U.S. at the end of 19th century. And Japan came to save Philippine people. That's a good work, good job!

---

* Just after the outbreak of the Pacific War, the Japanese military aimed for the capture of the Philippines, which was then an American colony. The U.S. and the Philippine forces were forced to withdraw from Manila. Douglas MacArthur, who was the commander, left the Philippines in Mar. 1942, the year after the outbreak of the war, and fled for Australia.

ドゥテルテ守護霊　ああ。

及川　第二次世界大戦をどうご覧になっておられますか。あなたのご意見は。

ドゥテルテ守護霊　ああ……。日本の勝利は立派なものだった。日本は、あと少しのところで勝利を逃がしたな。日本軍はあの時点でマッカーサー司令官を殺すべきだった（注）。あそこがポイントだね。

及川　そうですね。まさに、おっしゃる通りです。私たちは、あの戦争は白人国家からのアジアの独立革命だったと信じています。そう思われませんか。

ドゥテルテ守護霊　うーん……。われわれは19世紀の終わりにアメリカに占領された。日本はフィリピン人を救いに来た。立派に、よくやってくれたよ！　マッカーサー

（注）太平洋戦争の開戦直後、日本軍は、当時アメリカの植民地であったフィリピン攻略を目標としていた。米比軍は首都マニラからの撤退を余儀なくされ、司令官であるマッカーサーは開戦翌年の1942年3月フィリピンを脱出、オーストラリアに向かった。

And General MacArthur ran away to Australia. He's not a samurai. He should *Seppuku* suicide at the time. He's not a samurai. He's bad, and in addition to that, he dropped the atomic bomb, Hiroshima and Nagasaki. They are Hitler-like people. Hmm.

5 The Guardian Spirit Reveals His True Thinking on China

"We need Japan to protect weak countries of Asia"

Ayaori So, I'm wondering what is your opinion about Sino-Japanese War.

Duterte's G.S. Oh?

Ayaori Chinese-Japanese War.

司令官はオーストラリアへ逃げていった。あれはサムライじゃないね。あの時、切腹自殺するべきだったのに。サムライじゃない。悪人で、おまけに原爆を落とした、広島と長崎だ。ヒットラー並みの連中だよ、うん。

5　ドゥテルテ守護霊、中国に対する本心を明かす

「日本にアジアの弱い国々を守ってほしい」

綾織　日中戦争についてのご意見を伺いたいのですが。

ドゥテルテ守護霊　はい？

綾織　日中戦争です。

5 The Guardian Spirit Reveals His True Thinking on China

Duterte's G.S. Chinese-Japanese War?

Ayaori Yes.

Duterte's G.S. You mean before *Daitoa Senso* War?

Ayaori Yes.

Duterte's G.S. China and Japan?

Ayaori Yes.

Duterte's G.S. Hmm...

Ayaori What is your side?

Duterte's G.S. Japan came to China to save Manchuria. And Mao Tse-tung was a very coward person and he always ran away from Japanese army deep into the south part of China. He's a coward and

5　ドゥテルテ守護霊、中国に対する本心を明かす

ドゥテルテ守護霊　日中戦争？

綾織　はい。

ドゥテルテ守護霊　大東亜戦争の前の？

綾織　はい。

ドゥテルテ守護霊　中国と日本の？

綾織　はい。

ドゥテルテ守護霊　うーん……。

綾織　どちら側につきますか。

ドゥテルテ守護霊　日本は満州を救うために中国に来た。毛沢東（もうたくとう）は、とんだ臆病者（おくびょうもの）で、日本軍から中国南部の奥まで逃げてばかりいた。あれは臆病者で、英雄なんかじゃないよ。あんな奴の軍功なんか認めるわけにはいかん。偶然、

5 The Guardian Spirit Reveals His True Thinking on China

he's not a hero. I cannot agree with his military award. It's just by chance he received his fruits. Japan should perish Chinese communist party.

Ayaori Uh-huh.

Duterte's G.S. I think so. They are now growing bigger and bigger. And they are threatening us, Philippine people. We don't have enough army to fight against them. So, we need Japanese help. But we hate American aids. They are intruders, so we hate America. So, Japan should stand up by herself and protect not only Japan, but also other weak countries of Asia. This is the Japanese destination.

Oikawa Including your country?

Duterte's G.S. Yeah, of course. Of course. It's Japan. Japan can, could kill General MacArthur.

5　ドゥテルテ守護霊、中国に対する本心を明かす

成果を手に入れただけだから。日本は中国共産党を滅ぼさなきゃ駄目だ。

綾織　はい。

ドゥテルテ守護霊　そう思うね。中国は今、どんどん大きくなって、フィリピン国民を脅かしている。われわれには彼らと戦うだけの軍隊がないんで、日本の助けが必要なんです。アメリカに助けてもらうのは嫌だしね。アメリカは侵略者だから好かんのだ。だから日本は自分で立ち上がって、日本だけでなく他のアジアの弱い国々も守るべきだ。それが日本の目指すところだ。

及川　あなたの国も含めて？

ドゥテルテ守護霊　当然、そうだ。日本だよ。日本なら、マッカーサー司令官を殺すことができたんだ。

5 The Guardian Spirit Reveals His True Thinking on China

The money from China is the rental fee of South China Sea?

Ayaori You mentioned that the Philippines relies on China. You said that.

Duterte's G.S. Yeah.

Ayaori But that is not your true thought. Is it?

Duterte's G.S. They gave a lot of money, so…haha… I said so. But it is effective within my presidency. So, it's no more than 10 years. We got 2.5 *cho* [trillion] yen, so it's great. More than half of our national budget*. So, it's our rental fee of our South China…

Oikawa South China Sea?

---

* The national budget of the Philippines was approximately 2 trillion pesos in 2013, 2.3 trillion pesos in 2014, and 2.6 trillion pesos in 2015. The exchange rate on November 1, 2016, was 1 PHP≈2.17 JPY.

5　ドゥテルテ守護霊、中国に対する本心を明かす

中国からの支援金は「南シナ海の〝レンタル料〟」?

綾織　フィリピンは中国を頼りにしていると言われましたよね。

ドゥテルテ守護霊　ああ。

綾織　それは本心ではないというわけですか。

ドゥテルテ守護霊　中国は、たんまり金をくれたからさ。ハハ。だからそう言ったまでだ。まあ、私が大統領でいる間、有効なだけで、10年以上は続かないから。2.5兆円もくれたのは、すごいことだ。わが国の国家予算の半分以上だ（注）。南シナ海の〝レンタル料〟だよ。

及川　南シナ海の?

（注）フィリピンの国家予算は2013年度が約2兆ペソ、2014年度約2.3兆ペソ、2015年度約2.6兆ペソ。2016年11月1日時点のレートは1ペソ≒2.17円。

Duterte's G.S. Yeah, yeah, yeah, yeah. Rental fee. Rental. [*Laughs*.] So, it's good for 10 years.

Ayaori But it will not be rental.

Duterte's G.S. Rental. Just rental.

Ayaori No, I don't think so.

Duterte's G.S. After that, we'll attack them and get their buildings and their ships, of course, with the aid of Japan.

Sakakibara When you met Xi Jinping the other day, you were chewing a gum.

Duterte's G.S. Chewing a gum?

Sakakibara Yeah.

ドゥテルテ守護霊　そう、そう。〝レンタル料〟よ（笑）。だから、10年間は、いいんだよ。

綾織　レンタルにはなりませんよ。

ドゥテルテ守護霊　レンタルだよ。ただのレンタル。

綾織　いえ、そうは思えませんが。

ドゥテルテ守護霊　その後で中国を攻撃して、当然、ビルや船を奪う。日本の助けを得て。

榊原　先日、習近平と会われた時には、ガムを噛んでいましたね。

ドゥテルテ守護霊　ガムを噛んだ？

榊原　はい。

5 The Guardian Spirit Reveals His True Thinking on China

Duterte's G.S. Aaahhh!

Sakakibara So, what was your real intention in doing that?

Duterte's G.S. At that time, I don't know the reason but General MacArthur came to me and he advocated that "Please chew a gum and you'll look like General MacArthur." He said so. So, I pretended.

Oikawa What was your impression of Mr. Xi Jinping?

5　ドゥテルテ守護霊、中国に対する本心を明かす

ドゥテルテ守護霊　ああ！

榊原　本当は何を考えて、そうされたのでしょうか。

ドゥテルテ守護霊　あの時、なぜかマッカーサー司令官が私のところに来て、「ガムを噛んでください。そうすればマッカーサー司令官みたいに見えますから」と勧めてくれてね。だから、そんな振りをしたんだよ。

及川　習近平氏の印象はいかがでしたか。

2016年10月20日、北京訪問中に習近平主席と会談するドゥテルテ大統領（写真左）。

On October 20, 2016, President Duterte met with President Xi Jinping during his visit to Beijing (left).

Duterte's G.S. He's a... he has poor mind and... Oh! Oh!! I cannot say bad things. So, he is bigger than I. It's great.

He is just dealing with China to get money

Oikawa But you don't like Chinese communist, do you?

Duterte's G.S. Huh?

Oikawa You don't like Chinese communist.

Duterte's G.S. Chinese communism...China has two faces. Superficially, they say that they have loyalty to communism but in reality, they have a habit of gathering money, day by day. It's a money-earning country, so in reality, it's a capitalism. They have two faces. We cannot believe in their political policy. So, we must have the same attitude. We must have respect

ドゥテルテ守護霊　彼は心が貧（まず）しいし……おっと！　悪口言っちゃいけないんだった。彼は私より大きいから、立派なもんだよ。

中国とは、金をもらうために取り引きしているだけ

及川　でも、中国の共産主義者はお好きではないですよね。

ドゥテルテ守護霊　うん？

及川　中国の共産主義者がお好きではないと。

ドゥテルテ守護霊　中国の共産主義ねえ……。中国には二つの顔があって、表面的には共産主義に忠実だと言ってるけど、実際は毎日、お金集めが習慣になってる。「金儲けの国」であって、実際は資本主義だからね。二つの顔があるから、中国の政策は信用するわけにはいかなくて、こちらも同じ態度で行くしかない。中国に敬意は払うけど、その一方では……ああ、悪い言葉だな。それはそれとして、

to China. And another side, we must dis...dis...oh, bad words. By the way, we must respect Japan.

Oikawa OK.

Duterte's G.S. OK, OK, OK.

Oikawa So, you are so realistic that you are just dealing with China to get money, right?

Duterte's G.S. Oh, yeah, that's right. Yeah.

Oikawa So, you are not pro-Chinese.

Duterte's G.S. Huh?

Oikawa You are not pro-Chinese.

Duterte's G.S. Pro-Chinese? What? What English is that?

5　ドゥテルテ守護霊、中国に対する本心を明かす

日本を尊敬しないといけない。

及川　はい。

ドゥテルテ守護霊　そう、そう、そう。

及川　では、非常に現実主義者でいらっしゃるわけですね。中国とは、金をもらうために取り引きしているだけだと？

ドゥテルテ守護霊　ああ、そう。その通り。うん。

及川　では、親中派ではないわけですね。

ドゥテルテ守護霊　うん？

及川　あなたは親中ではないと。

ドゥテルテ守護霊　Pro-Chinese？それはどういう英語かな。

5 The Guardian Spirit Reveals His True Thinking on China

Oikawa You don't like China?

Duterte's G.S. Oh... my mother came from China, so...

Oikawa Mother's grandparents?

Duterte's G.S. Yeah, like that. So, I don't hate them. Only I ask them to give money. That's all.

Oikawa OK.

Duterte's G.S. It's just a Chinese main policy or Chinese mentality, hmm...to be Chinese means to love money more than life. It's Chinese, OK? To be Japanese means love money next to life. It's the difference.

Oikawa Very interesting.

5　ドゥテルテ守護霊、中国に対する本心を明かす

及川　あなたは、中国が好きではないと。

ドゥテルテ守護霊　ああ……私の母は中国の出だから……。

及川　お母様の祖父母、ですか。

ドゥテルテ守護霊　ああ、その辺かな。だから中国人は嫌いじゃない。「金をくれ」と頼むだけだ。それだけだよ。

及川　分かりました。

ドゥテルテ守護霊　それこそ、まさに中国人の基本方針であり、中国人のメンタリティーなんで。中国人であるということは、「命よりお金が大事」ということだ。それが中国人なのよ。分かる？　日本人であるということは、「命の次にお金が大事」ということで、そこの違いだな。

及川　実に興味深いお話です。

5 The Guardian Spirit Reveals His True Thinking on China

Sakakibara So, Chinese people, especially the communist people, believe in materialism. And people in the Philippines don't like materialism because they believe in God. So…

Duterte's G.S. God, believe in God.

Sakakibara So, you will agree with people in the Philippines?

Duterte's G.S. Huh?

Sakakibara So, you have the same faith in God. So, you hate materialism?

Duterte's G.S. What do you mean by materialism? If you mean, materialism mean paper money and coin, we are materialism.

Sakakibara Ah, no, no. Materialism denies the

榊原　ですから中国人、特に共産党員たちは唯物論を信じています。フィリピン人は唯物論は好きではありません。神を信じているからです。では……。

ドゥテルテ守護霊　神だよ。神を信じている。

榊原　では、あなたもフィリピンの人たちと同じご意見ですか。

ドゥテルテ守護霊　うん？

榊原　あなたも同じく神を信じていらっしゃるので、唯物論は嫌いであると？

ドゥテルテ守護霊　唯物論って、どういう意味？　唯物論とは、お札やコインのことだというなら、私たちは唯物論だけど。

榊原　いえいえ、唯物論は、神の存在を否定します。

existence of God.

Duterte's G.S. Ah, really?

Sakakibara Yeah.

Duterte's G.S. Materialism means bread and money or...

Sakakibara Because we need that for living. But basically, communist people don't believe in God.

Duterte's G.S. Oh... Why?

Sakakibara So, that's the problem.

Duterte's G.S. Ah... Because Xi Jinping is a replacement of God. Of course, Duterte is God, so almost the same. But Duterte is a God of Jesus Christ, so the situation is a little different.

ドゥテルテ守護霊　えっ、そうなのか。

榊原　はい。

ドゥテルテ守護霊　唯物論とは「パンとお金」のことで……。

榊原　生きていくためには、それらが必要です。しかし、基本的に共産主義者は神を信じていません。

ドゥテルテ守護霊　おお……何で？

榊原　ですから、そこが問題なのです。

ドゥテルテ守護霊　ああ……習近平が〝神の代わり〟だからか。もちろんドゥテルテも〝神〟だから、ほぼ同じだな。ドゥテルテは〝イエス・キリストの神〟だから、少し事情が違うけど。

"The United States and Great Britain should apologize to Asian people"

Sakakibara OK. And so, while you express that you are supportive to China, on the other hand, you speak ill of Americans. The people are so afraid that American people will go away from the Philippines, especially business people and developers.

Duterte's G.S. Uh-huh.

Sakakibara Yeah. That means, in a sense, the economy in the Philippines will decline. That's what we are afraid of. So, what do you think about that?

Duterte's G.S. American people did nothing for the Philippines. It's the same as Okinawa. Okinawan people went mad because of American military forces. They are Japanese, but they are not Japanese. They are not Chinese, but they want to be Chinese. I understand.

5　ドゥテルテ守護霊、中国に対する本心を明かす

米英はアジアの人々に謝罪すべき

榊原　はい。そして、あなたは中国を支持すると表明しつつ、一方でアメリカ人を悪く言っています。特にビジネスをやっている人や開発業者は、アメリカ人がフィリピンからいなくなるのではないかと懸念(けねん)しています。

ドゥテルテ守護霊　うーん。

榊原　はい。それはある意味、フィリピン経済が落ち込んでいくということではないかと、私たちは懸念しております。この点はどう思われますか。

ドゥテルテ守護霊　アメリカ人はフィリピンのために何もしてないよ。沖縄と同じだから。沖縄の人たちはアメリカ軍に怒り狂った。沖縄の人たちは日本人であって日本人でないからね。中国人でもないけど、中国人になりたがってる。それは分かる。アメリカの政策が沖縄の人たちを怒ら

American policy changed people into becoming mad. Like the Great Britain changed India into very poor country and made them under human being. So they, both Great Britain and the United States, are very bad. They have been very bad. They should apologize to Asian people. Japan is the only savior for us and the last hope for us. So, I declared Mr. Abe, *bimbo* Abe, we are standing in the same side. We are friends.

Sakakibara I see.

6 His Outlook on the South China Sea Problem with China

Both the Philippines and Japan must cut the leash

Ayaori So, in Beijing, you stated that the Philippines would break away from the U.S. What did you mean

せたんだ。大英帝国がインドをひどく貧しい国にして、人間以下の存在にしたのと同じことだ。だから大英帝国もアメリカも、どちらも相当ひどい。相当ひどいことをしてきたんで、アジアの人々に謝罪すべきだ。日本だけが「われわれの救世主」であり、「最後の希望」なんだよ。だから私は安倍さんに、貧乏な安倍さんに、日本の味方だと宣言した。われわれは友人なんだから。

榊原　分かりました。

6　中国との南シナ海問題の見通しは？

フィリピンも日本も「紐」を切らなければならない

綾織　北京では、「フィリピンはアメリカと決別する」と言われましたが、それはどういう意味だったのでしょうか。

by that?

Duterte's G.S. I hate Obama.

Ayaori Will you leave from the U.S. economically and militarily?

Duterte's G.S. Ah, it's recommendable policy. We must have our own independent policy. If we are not independent, we are not one nation, one country, we rely on Japan first, next China, and America is lower than third.

Oikawa So, let me confirm. Are you going to protect your country without U.S. troops?

Duterte's G.S. U.S. troops are occupying us. We are not a dog on leash, you know? Dog on leash. It's American policy. We must cut the chain, the leash. Japan also. Japan must become independent. Japan is

ドゥテルテ守護霊　オバマは嫌いだから。

綾織　では、経済的にも軍事的にもアメリカから離れていくと？

ドゥテルテ守護霊　ああ、それが望ましい政策だね。自分たちの独立政策を持たないと駄目だ。仮にフィリピンが独立しておらず、一つの国民、一つの国家でないとしたら、まずは日本を頼り、次に中国を頼るだろうね。アメリカは三番目以下だ。

及川　では、確認させてください。あなたは、米軍なしで自国を守るつもりなのでしょうか。

ドゥテルテ守護霊　米軍は私たちを占領してるんだよ。私らは紐に繋がれた犬なんかじゃない。分かる？　「犬を紐に繋いでおく」のがアメリカの政策なんだ。鎖を、紐を切らなきゃ駄目だ。日本だってそうだろう。日本も独立しな

a greater country than now. You are. So, we expect you and when the Chinese Xi Jinping gave us 250,000 billion yen to us, Japan must give 500 thousand billion yen to us. Twice. You understand? *Go cho-en*. Go cho-en. You know? You know? It's Japanese amount. *Goju oku*? No, no, no, *sukunai*.

Oikawa So, you expect much more money from Japan?

Duterte's G.S. It's *tetsuke* [deposit], tetsuke, tetsuke. You know?

Oikawa OK, OK. I have another question about the Philippines god. So, about 20 years ago, Mount Pinatubo had an eruption.

Duterte's G.S. Mount Pinatubo's eru…

Oikawa Mount Pinatubo's explosion. And that became

けりゃ駄目だ。日本は本来、今のあり方よりも偉大な国なんだ。本当だよ。だから君たちには期待してる。中国の習近平が２兆５千億円くれるなら、日本は倍の５兆円くれないと。分かる？　５兆円だよ、ゴチョウエン。分かる？　分かってる？　それが日本の額だろう。50億？　駄目、駄目、駄目、少ない。

及川　では、日本から、もっと多くの金額を期待されていると？

ドゥテルテ守護霊　手付(てつけ)だよ。手付。手付金。分かるかな？

及川　はい、分かりました。フィリピンの神について、もう一つ質問があります。20年ほど前、ピナツボ山が噴火しました。

ドゥテルテ守護霊　ピナツボ山が噴……。

及川　爆発しました。それが、米軍がフィリピンを撤退す

the reason the U.S. army left the Philippines. So, do you have any relations with the Mount Pinatubo's explosion?

Duterte's G.S. [*Laughs.*] Ha, ha, ha. Oh, you go to hospital. [*Audience laugh.*] You should.

Oikawa Why?

Duterte's G.S. We are realistic. We are realistic, so we are not dreamers. We don't need any illusion.

Oikawa So, you didn't need the U.S. in the Philippines?

Duterte's G.S. Pinatubo. OK. Now just kill bad people and make a country for a good direction and become wealthy. And we, Japan, China should make a new colleague, colleague for Asia. A new EU for Asian people. It's good. America should go back to America.

る理由となりました。そこで、ピナツボ山の噴火とは、何か関係がおありなのでしょうか。

ドゥテルテ守護霊　(笑)ハハハ。ああ、病院に行けよ(会場笑)。行ったほうがいい。

及川　なぜですか。

ドゥテルテ守護霊　私たちは現実主義者なんだ。現実主義者であって夢想家(むそうか)じゃない。幻想なんて必要ないんで。

及川　では、フィリピンにアメリカは必要ないと？

ドゥテルテ守護霊　ピナツボ山か。オーケー。今は、とにかく悪人を殺して、国を良い方向へ導いて豊かになること。われわれと日本と中国は新たな仲間になるべきだ。アジアのための仲間。アジアの人々のための新たなEU。それがいい。アメリカはアメリカに帰るべきだ。

6 His Outlook on the South China Sea Problem with China

He wants to improve the safety in the Philippines and invite Japanese capitals

Sakakibara So, do you have any idea how you can solve the problem of the South China Sea?

Duterte's G.S. South China Sea? If we can get rental fee, it's OK.

Sakakibara OK, so you think it is the Philippines' territory originally?

Duterte's G.S. Originally.

Sakakibara And if China forcefully invaded and ruled that area, what would you do about it?

Duterte's G.S. But after I made a visit to Beijing, our fishing boat became safe. In addition to that, I borrowed two more big Japanese patrolling ships. It's to protect

フィリピンの治安を良くして
日本の資本を招き入れたい

榊原　では、南シナ海の問題をどう解決するか、何かお考えはありますか。

ドゥテルテ守護霊　南シナ海？〝レンタル料〟をもらえればオーケーだ。

榊原　分かりました。南シナ海は本来、フィリピンの領土であると思われますか。

ドゥテルテ守護霊　本来はそうだ。

榊原　もし、中国が強引に侵略して、その地域を支配したら、どうされますか。

ドゥテルテ守護霊　だが、私が北京を訪問した後で、フィリピンの漁船は安全になったし、さらに、日本の大型巡視船をもう2隻(せき)借りることができた。中国の戦艦などから漁

our fishing people from China, Chinese battleship or like that. So, I made it perfect.

Sakakibara I see.

Oikawa Did you talk about that with Mr. Abe?

Duterte's G.S. ?

Oikawa Did you talk about what you said right now about the South China Sea problem with Mr. Abe?

Duterte's G.S. He just asked me, "Please understand our situation." He said it just like that. Mr. Abe was very afraid of having Barack Obama acknowledge the total amount of helping us, so he wanted to hide the amount. Under the table, he gave me a promise. It's more helpful for Filipinos to make a promise with Japan because it has a lot of money. We want to use more and more money every year. So, if I kill bad people in the Philippines and

民を守るためだよ。だから、私は完璧(かんぺき)にやったな。

榊原　なるほど。

及川　安倍さんとは、その話をしましたか。

ドゥテルテ守護霊　？

及川　今おっしゃった南シナ海の問題を、安倍さんと話し合いましたか。

ドゥテルテ守護霊　彼は、「どうか、こちらの立場を分かってください」と頼んできたよ。そんなことを言ってたな。安倍さんは、日本が援助してくれている総額をバラク・オバマに知られるのを、すごく恐れていて、その金額を隠したがってた。〝テーブルの下〞では約束してくれたさ。フィリピンの人たちは、日本と約束するほうが得だ。日本は金持ちだからね。私たちは毎年もっともっとお金を使いたいんで、私がフィリピンの悪人を殺して、安全な都市、安全

made a safe city, safe country, Japan can build a lot of factories and industries. And UNIQLO will come to the Philippines from China and we will make prosperity. Under the table we shook hands with Mr. Abe. Mr. Abe and Philippine president, yeah.

So, China is now expanding, but in reality, they don't have enough money. I know about that. Japan has real money, affluent money by Kuroda Nichigin General, so we can receive more money. We have...

Oikawa I see, I see. But you know, coming back to the South China Sea, if China successfully invades the Scarborough Reef, that would be a big problem, not only for your country, but also for Japan.

Duterte's G.S. No, no, no, no, no, we'll lose fishing rights. But they made a promise that they will buy our banana instead of fish. So, it's OK.

Oikawa Is it enough?

な国を創れば、日本は工場や産業をたくさん作れるし、ユニクロは中国からフィリピンに移転して、フィリピンは繁栄していける。〝テーブルの下〟では安倍さんと手を握ってるんだよ、安倍さんとフィリピンの大統領が。

　中国は今、拡大しつつあるけれど、実際には、あまり金がないことは分かってる。日本は黒田日銀総裁のおかげで、お金が現実に豊富にあるから、私たちは、より多くお金がもらえる。そして……。

及川　分かりました。しかし、南シナ海の件に戻りますが、もし中国がスカボロー礁への侵略に成功したら、あなたの国だけでなく日本にとっても大きな問題になるでしょう。

ドゥテルテ守護霊　いやいや、漁業権は失うが、魚の代わりにバナナを買う約束をしてくれたよ。だから大丈夫。

及川　それで十分なのですか。

Duterte's G.S. Enough, enough, enough, enough.

"We don't need to protect our sea"

Sakakibara How about securing the route of oil?

Duterte's G.S. Hmm?

Sakakibara Yeah, oil. Importing the oil. So…

Duterte's G.S. Importing the oil.

Sakakibara That's…

Duterte's G.S. Japanese Self-Defense Army will be active in the near future, so it's OK. No problem. We'll support you.

Ayaori At this point, it's not possible.

ドゥテルテ守護霊　十分、十分、十分、十分。

領海は「守らなくても大丈夫」？

榊原　石油輸入ルートの確保についてはいかがですか。

ドゥテルテ守護霊　うん？

榊原　ええ、石油です。石油の輸入です。

ドゥテルテ守護霊　石油の輸入ねえ。

榊原　それは……。

ドゥテルテ守護霊　日本の自衛隊が近い将来、活動を増すから、大丈夫だよ。問題ない。私たちも支持するから。

綾織　今の時点では不可能ですよ。

Duterte's G.S. Oh, really?

Ayaori Yeah.

Duterte's G.S. It's OK, it's OK, it's OK.

Ayaori Japan will not be able to deal with military conflict in the South China Sea so quickly.

Duterte's G.S. At that time, we'll buy coal from Australia, Mongolia district. And we have solar panel.

Oikawa So, the U.S. will leave your country and Japan cannot send our troops to your area. So, without the U.S. and Japan, how do you protect your sea?

Duterte's G.S. Ah, OK, OK. We don't need to protect our sea. We don't think it's a problem. Sea is not a problem. Problem is fish. Fish are swimming from

ドゥテルテ守護霊　ああ、そうなのか？

綾織　はい。

ドゥテルテ守護霊　大丈夫、大丈夫、大丈夫。

綾織　日本は南シナ海での軍事紛争に、それ程、迅速(じんそく)には動けませんので。

ドゥテルテ守護霊　そうなったら、オーストラリアやモンゴルから石炭を買うよ。ソーラーパネルも持ってるし。

及川　アメリカはフィリピンから離れていくでしょうし、日本はフィリピンの領域に部隊を送ることはできません。アメリカや日本の支援なしで、どうやって領海を守るのですか。

ドゥテルテ守護霊　ああ、大丈夫、大丈夫。領海なんて守らなくてもいいのよ。そんなの問題とは思っていない。問題は海じゃなくて魚だ。魚は中国からフィリピンやベトナ

China to the Philippines, Vietnam, Japan, all around the world. So, they cannot have nationality. Fish don't have nationality. So, we will do another... China has a great population, so they need fish, I understand. Japan also. But Japan has new technology for breeding fish artificially. So, we don't have much. It's OK. Around the Philippines, there are a lot of fish, so no problem.

Sakakibara So, you think like that because the Philippines is mainly dependent on the first stage industry. OK.

Oikawa So, you're really comfortable with the promise with China, so you allow to do the fishing?

Duterte's G.S. Because they gave us two-thirds of their national budget in my one visit. My second visit will be crucial for them. Hahaha!

Ayaori But I think it's possible that China will invade

ムや日本や世界中に泳いでいって、国籍なんて持ちようがない。魚に国籍はないんで、われわれがするのは何か別の……。中国は巨大な人口を抱えているから、魚が必要なのは分かる。日本もそうだけど、日本には人工的に魚を養殖する新技術がある。だから、十分にはないけど大丈夫。フィリピンの周りには魚がたくさんいるし、問題ない。

榊原　フィリピンは主に第一次産業に依存しているので、そうお考えなのですね。分かりました。

及川　本当に中国との約束に不安はないわけですか。だから中国に漁業を許すと。

ドゥテルテ守護霊　だって、私が一回訪問したら国家予算の3分の2ほどのお金を出してくれたし。二度目に訪問したら、どえらいことになるだろうよ。ハハハ！

綾織　中国がサンゴ礁の島々だけではなく、フィリピン本

your country. Not only the reef islands, but your main land will be intruded.

Duterte's G.S. At that time, I will be the president of China.

Ayaori Oh, really?

Duterte's G.S. Because I can kill bad people. I'm stronger than Xi Jinping.

7 The Guardian Spirit's Vision of the Asian Century

He is "the god of mercy inviting inferno for the United States"

Sakakibara So, where are your firm beliefs or thinking, to kill or punish to improve or bring peace,

土を侵略してくることもありうると思いますが。

ドゥテルテ守護霊　その時は、私が中国の国家主席になってるから。

綾織　おお、本当ですか。

ドゥテルテ守護霊　私は悪人たちを殺すことができるんで、習近平より強いからね。

7　「アジアの世紀」のビジョンを語る　　ドゥテルテ守護霊

「アメリカに地獄をもたらす慈悲の神」を自称

榊原　「殺したり罰したりすることによって物事が改善したり、平和がもたらされる」というあなたの固い信念は、どの

coming from? From your depths of your soul?

Duterte's G.S. Hmm...

Sakakibara So, you're the god of punishment?

Duterte's G.S. Ah, no, no. Mercy. Of course. God of mercy is inviting new inferno for the United States. They did bad things in these 100 years, so they need to apologize to Asian people. Of course, European people must apologize to African and Asian people or Indian people.

Next age will be the age of China and India. So, it means the age of Asia. And we have good friendship with India and China. These two countries have almost half of the population of the world. So, next is the Asian century.

Sakakibara I see. Has it already been decided in Heaven that you were going to be the president of the Philippines?

ような考え方から来るのでしょうか。魂の奥底からですか。

ドゥテルテ守護霊　うーん……。

榊原　あなたは「罰する神」なのですか。

ドゥテルテ守護霊　いや、違う。もちろん「慈悲」だよ。「慈悲の神」がアメリカに〝新たな地獄〟をもたらしているわけだ。彼らはここ100年間、悪いことをしてきたから、アジアの人たちに謝罪する必要がある。もちろん、ヨーロッパ人はアフリカやアジア、インドの人たちに謝罪しないといけない。

　次の時代は、中国とインドの時代になる。つまり、アジアの時代だよ。そして、われわれはインドと中国と友好関係にある。この二国で世界の人口のほぼ半分を占めるわけだから、次は「アジアの世紀」なんだ。

榊原　分かりました。あなたがフィリピンの大統領になることは、天上界ですでに決められていたのでしょうか。

Duterte's G.S. Huh?

Sakakibara In Heaven, has it already been decided or planned that you're going to be the president of the Philippines at this time? Is it God's plan?

Duterte's G.S. You know, I'm the Ironman and I'm the Batman of the American hero who descended to the Philippines. So, I'm a hero. Hero of the people. So, they supported me about 90 percent. You understand? 90 percent!

Sakakibara Yes, yes. I heard about that.

Duterte's G.S. Almost 90 percent.

Sakakibara Extraordinary rate.

Duterte's G.S. It's a God. Nearly equal to God.

ドゥテルテ守護霊　うん？

榊原　この時期に、あなたがフィリピンの大統領になるということは、天上界ですでに決められていた、あるいは予定されていたのでしょうか。神の計画でしょうか。

ドゥテルテ守護霊　だから、私はフィリピンに降臨した、アメリカン・ヒーローの〝アイアンマン〟であり〝バットマン〟なのよ。ヒーローだ。人々のヒーローなんだ。フィリピン人の約90パーセントが私を支持してる。分かってる？　90パーセントよ！

榊原　はい、お伺いしています。

ドゥテルテ守護霊　ほぼ90パーセントだからね。

榊原　ものすごい率ですね。

ドゥテルテ守護霊　〝神〟だな。ほぼ、〝神そのもの〟だ。

Oikawa I understand that you are a hero. But you know, it seems your way of thinking is based on nationalism rather than globalism.

Duterte's G.S. Nationalism?

Oikawa Now, most of the world leaders are globalist.

Duterte's G.S. Globalist.

Oikawa For example, Obama is a globalist. But you are purely nationalist. So, that's a difference.

Duterte's G.S. I'm the president of the Philippines, so I must think, "Philippines first" like "American first."

Oikawa Philippines first?

Duterte's G.S. They think America first. We think

7 「アジアの世紀」のビジョンを語るドゥテルテ守護霊

及川　あなたがヒーローであることは分かりますが、あなたの考え方は、グローバリズムというよりナショナリズムに基づいているように思われます。

ドゥテルテ守護霊　ナショナリズム？

及川　今日、世界のリーダーの多くはグローバリストです。

ドゥテルテ守護霊　グローバリスト。

及川　たとえばオバマはグローバリストですが、あなたは純然たるナショナリストですので、そこが違っています。

ドゥテルテ守護霊　私はフィリピンの大統領だから、「アメリカ第一」と同じで、「フィリピン第一」に考えないといかんからな。

及川　フィリピン第一ですか。

ドゥテルテ守護霊　彼らは「アメリカ第一」の考えで、わ

Philippines first.

"Trump will let Japan go as an Asian leader"

Ayaori In the U.S., presidential election is coming. What do you think about the candidate Mr. Trump and Mrs. Clinton?

Duterte's G.S. Mr. Trump says America first and Hillary will continue the next Obama, Obama the 2nd like that. So, Trump will be better because he will let Japan go as an Asian leader, so it will be helpful for us. Japan-Philippine relationship is very good. We are friends. We cannot break our promise. So, I rely on Japanese people.

American troops did bad things, but they never revealed that kind of bad deed and they condemn other countries only. Japan or Germany or Italy, like that. But they have their own intention to intrude us. They are at the opposite side of the Earth. They should not come

れらは「フィリピン第一」だ。

「トランプなら日本をアジアのリーダーにしてくれる」

綾織　アメリカでは大統領選挙が近づいていますが、トランプ候補とクリントン候補について、どう思われますか。

ドゥテルテ守護霊　トランプさんは「アメリカ第一」と言ってるけど、ヒラリーはオバマ路線を引き継いで第二のオバマみたいにやるだろうから、トランプのほうがいいだろう。日本をアジアのリーダーにしてくれるだろうから、私たちにとっても助かる。日比関係は非常に良好で、友人同士だからね。約束を破ることはできない。日本人が頼りなんだよ。

　米軍は悪いことをしても、そういう悪行を絶対に表沙汰にせず、日本やドイツやイタリアとか他国を非難するばかりだけど、彼らこそ、われわれを侵略する意図がある。地球の反対側にいるんだから、アジアに来るべきじゃないんだ。ハワイは彼らの国じゃない。ハワイは日本に差し出す

to Asia. Hawaii is not their country. They should give Hawaii to Japan. Japanese colony first, I think so.

Oikawa So, you don't like Obama, but you prefer Trump?

Duterte's G.S. Yeah. He's good. He just has concern about building new Trump Tower only, so it's good [*audience laugh*] for him and for us.

Oikawa OK. So, if Trump wins the election, do you think you can create a new relationship with the U.S.?

Duterte's G.S. No, no. We make new relationship with Japan, and Japan will remake the relationship with the U.S. It's enough.

べきだ。まずは〝日本の植民地〟だと思うけどね。

及川　では、オバマのことはお好きでなく、トランプがお好きということでしょうか。

ドゥテルテ守護霊　そうだよ。彼はいいね。彼は新しいトランプ・タワーを建てることにしか関心がないから、いいんだよ。（会場笑）彼にとっても私たちにとっても。

及川　分かりました。では、もしトランプ氏が選挙に勝利した場合、アメリカとは新たな関係を築けるとお考えですか。

ドゥテルテ守護霊　いや、いや。私たちは日本と新たな関係を築いて、日本がアメリカと関係をつくり直せば、それで十分。

7 The Guardian Spirit's Vision of the Asian Century

Suggesting Japanese as the official language of the new Asian economic area

Oikawa Maybe Trump will say, "The U.S. armies should leave other countries." So, Japan, the Philippines, and NATO. Are you happy to do that?

Duterte's G.S. We have small power now, so we don't have enough political power to say. But for example, the United Nations secretary-general, it's a Korean secretary-general... who was that?

Sakakibara Ban Ki-Moon?

Duterte's G.S. Ban Ki-Moon. Stupid Ban Ki-Moon. Under the stupid Ban Ki-Moon, there can be expected nothing. So, it cannot be expected nothing. So, we ask Japan, "Have leadership in Asian area. We can rely on." But America is far from us, so they don't understand our situation. They think we are one of the islands of China

7 「アジアの世紀」のビジョンを語るドゥテルテ守護霊

「日本語を公用語とする新・アジア経済圏」を提唱

及川　トランプ氏は、「アメリカ軍は他国から退(ひ)くべきだ」と言い出すでしょう。日本やフィリピンやＮＡＴＯからもです。それで結構なのでしょうか。

ドゥテルテ守護霊　フィリピンは、まだ小国で、政治的発言力が弱いけど、たとえば国連の事務総長、韓国人の事務総長、誰だっけ。

榊原　潘基文(パン・キムン)ですか？

ドゥテルテ守護霊　潘基文。潘基文の馬鹿。潘基文の馬鹿野郎のもとでは、何ひとつ期待できないから。期待できることはない。だから日本に、「アジア圏でリーダーシップをとってください。日本なら頼(たよ)れます」と頼んでるんだよ。アメリカは遠く離れてるから、こちらの状況なんか分からない。私たちを、中国の島の一つぐらいにしか思ってない。

or like that. They think like that. Obama especially doesn't understand the difference between Okinawa, Ishigaki, Senkaku, Taiwan, Scarborough Islands or around that, and Davao. He doesn't understand Davao.

Sakakibara I see.

Duterte's G.S. So, they are indifferent to us.

Sakakibara Yeah, of course. Yeah, I agree that America is far from Asia. But on the other hand, because of the American occupation in the Philippines, so many people are living in the United States doing their business. So, how do you care about those people in the United States?

Duterte's G.S. We are officially using English, but I think we should change our official language from English to Japanese. So, it's a greater future, I think. And China also must learn Japanese, it should be their

そんな考えなんだ。特にオバマは、沖縄も石垣島も、尖閣諸島も台湾もスカボロー礁やその周辺も、そしてダバオも区別がつかないから。ダバオのことなんか分からんから。

榊原　なるほど。

ドゥテルテ守護霊　私たちのことに関心なんてないんだよ。

榊原　ええ、そうですね。はい、確かにアメリカはアジアから離れています。しかし一方で、アメリカのフィリピン占領によって、アメリカに住んでビジネスをやっている人が数多くいます。そうした、アメリカにいる人たちのことは、どうされますか。

ドゥテルテ守護霊　フィリピンは英語を公用語として使ってるけど、英語から日本語に変えるべきなんだ。そのほうが、もっと素晴らしい未来になると思う。中国も日本語を習わないと。中国の公用語にすべきだし、インドも日本

official language. India also, use Japanese. Japanese trading area will have more than three or four billion people. It will make new economic area. We can survive.

Sakakibara We are happy to hear that.

Oikawa However, some of the Southeast Asian countries, like Cambodia, Laos, are going to China's zone, China's territory. What do you think about them?

Duterte's G.S. Hmm.

Oikawa We are afraid the Philippines will belong to China, like Cambodia and Laos.

Duterte's G.S. OK, OK, after that, Japanese army will occupy Beijing, so it's OK. No problem.

語を使うべきだね。そうすれば、日本の貿易圏は30億から40億人以上になって、新たな経済圏が生まれるだろう。それで生き残れる。

榊原　うれしいお言葉です。

及川　ただ、カンボジアやラオスのような東南アジアのいくつかの国は、中国圏、中国の領土になろうとしています。そうした国についてはどう思われますか。

ドゥテルテ守護霊　うーん。

及川　フィリピンも、カンボジアやラオスのように中国の属国になるのではないかと、心配なのですが。

ドゥテルテ守護霊　はい、はい。そうなったら日本軍が北京を占領してくれるから大丈夫です。問題ない。

8 Revealing His Deep Connection to Japan and Speaking in Japanese

"I have a shrine in Japan"

Sakakibara So, you do like Japan and Japanese. Are you spiritually connected to Japan?

Duterte's G.S. Of course, of course, of course.

Sakakibara Could you tell us about?

Duterte's G.S. Hmm?

Sakakibara About more…

Duterte's G.S. More?

Sakakibara Yeah, your strong ties.

8 日本との「深い縁」を明かし、 日本語で語り始める

「日本に私の神社がある」

榊原　日本と日本人が大好きでいらっしゃるんですね。日本と霊的な縁がおありなのでしょうか。

ドゥテルテ守護霊　それはもちろん、その通りです。

榊原　教えていただけますか。

ドゥテルテ守護霊　え？

榊原　それについて、もう少し。

ドゥテルテ守護霊　もっと？

榊原　はい、深い縁のところを。

8 Revealing His Deep Connection to Japan and Speaking in Japanese

Duterte's G.S. Ah, I was Japanese.

Sakakibara Really?

Duterte's G.S. Uh-huh.

Sakakibara Could you tell us the name of your past life?

Duterte's G.S. Past life?

Sakakibara Yeah, in Japanese.

Duterte's G.S. Ah, I forgot, but I have a shrine in Japan.

Sakakibara Oh, wow.

Ayaori Which era were you born in?

ドゥテルテ守護霊　ああ、もと日本人だから。

榊原　本当ですか。

ドゥテルテ守護霊　うん。

榊原　過去世(かこぜ)のお名前を教えていただけますか。

ドゥテルテ守護霊　過去世？

榊原　はい、日本人の時の。

ドゥテルテ守護霊　ああ、忘れたけど、日本に私の神社があるよ。

榊原　おお、すごい。

綾織　どの時代（era）に生まれていましたか。

8 Revealing His Deep Connection to Japan and Speaking in Japanese

Duterte's G.S. Hmm?

Ayaori Which *era*?

Duterte's G.S. Which *area*? Near here.

Oikawa & Ayaori Near here?

Sakakibara Near here?

Duterte's G.S. *Un* (Yeah).

Oikawa So, any related to the Philippines trade in the past Japanese history?

Duterte's G.S. No, I was a warrior of Japan or a general of Japan.

Interviewers Oh.

ドゥテルテ守護霊　うん？

綾織　どの時代ですか。

ドゥテルテ守護霊　どの地域（area）？　この近くだよ。

及川・綾織　この近く？

榊原　この近くですか。

ドゥテルテ守護霊　うん。

及川　すると、日本の過去の歴史で、フィリピン貿易に何か関係されていますか。

ドゥテルテ守護霊　いや、日本の武士、日本の将軍です。

質問者一同　おお。

Ayaori In World War II?

Duterte's G.S. Hmm...

Oikawa Before World War II?

Duterte's G.S. Un.

A past life as a great general during Japan-China War and Japan-Russia War

Oikawa One of the famous Japanese soldiers?

Duterte's G.S. Un.

Sakakibara Admiral Togo?

Duterte's G.S. Admiral Togo? Oh, not so bad. It's OK *yo*. Un. Not so bad. Not so bad. Very akin to him.

綾織　第二次世界大戦ですか。

ドゥテルテ守護霊　うーん……。

及川　第二次世界大戦前ですか？

ドゥテルテ守護霊　うん。

過去世は日清・日露戦争の、あの名将

及川　有名な日本の軍人のお一人ですか。

ドゥテルテ守護霊　うん。

榊原　東郷元帥(とうごうげんすい)ですか。

ドゥテルテ守護霊　東郷元帥？　うん、悪くないね。オーケーですよ。うん。悪くない、悪くない。彼に近いですね。

8 Revealing His Deep Connection to Japan and Speaking in Japanese

Sakaibara Ah, akin to him.

Ayaori In the Japanese-Russo War?

Duterte's G.S. Hmm?

Sakakibara Akin to him, ah, hmm.

Oikawa Which war in Japanese history did you join?

Duterte's G.S. Japan-China War, and Japan-Russia War.

Ayaori Oh, General Nogi*?

Duterte's G.S. Yeah.

Ayaori Oh, it's great. I admire you.

榊原　ああ、彼に近い。

綾織　日露戦争中ですか。

ドゥテルテ守護霊　うん？

榊原　似ている人、ああ、うーん。

及川　日本史の中の、どの戦争に参加されましたか。

ドゥテルテ守護霊　日清戦争と日露戦争です。

綾織　おお、乃木将軍（注）ですか。

ドゥテルテ守護霊　そうです。

綾織　おお、素晴らしい。敬服いたします。

8 Revealing His Deep Connection to Japan and Speaking in Japanese

Duterte's G.S. General Nogi is my past life.

（※以下、日本語による霊言の英訳）

OK, let's speak Japanese.

Ayaori [*Laughs.*] [*Audience laugh.*] Oh, my… [*laughs.*]

Duterte's G.S. I'm not good at English.

Ayaori [*Laughs.*] [*Audience laugh.*]

8　日本との「深い縁」を明かし、日本語で語り始める

ドゥテルテ守護霊　乃木将軍が私の過去世です。

（※以降、日本語での会話となる）

　じゃあ、日本語にしようか。

綾織　（笑）（会場笑）すごい（笑）。

ドゥテルテ守護霊　英語、苦手なんだ。

綾織　（笑）（会場笑）

（注）乃木希典（のぎまれすけ）（1849〜1912）長州藩出身の軍人で陸軍大将。第二次長州征伐で奇兵隊に参加し幕府軍と戦う。明治維新後は、西南戦争、日清戦争に出征。日露戦争では第三軍司令官として旅順攻略を指揮する。昭和天皇の教育係も務めた。明治天皇の大葬の日、妻とともに殉死。港区・赤坂など全国各地の「乃木神社」に祀られている。

* Maresuke Nogi (1849~1912) An officer from the Choshu feudal clan and a general in the Imperial Japanese Army. Participated in Kiheitai in the second Choshu conquest and fought against shogunate forces. After the Meiji Restoration, he went to the front of the Seinan War and the First Sino-Japanese War. He led the capture of Port Arthur as the commander of the Japanese Third Army in the Russo-Japanese War. He later became an education officer for Emperor Showa. On the day of the imperial funeral of Emperor Meiji, Nogi and his wife followed him to his grave. He is worshipped in Nogi Shrines all over Japan including the one in Akasaka of Minato Ward.

8 Revealing His Deep Connection to Japan and Speaking in Japanese

Duterte's G.S. If I don't speak English, International Headquarters cannot get money. [*Audience laugh.*] So, I'm trying my best.

Ayaori [*Laughs.*]

Duterte's G.S. It's too much. Japanese is OK. I want to say, "It's enough." [*Audience laugh.*] You know?

I'm mad at Japanese politics. Do you understand? [*To Ayaori.*] If I say in Japanese, you can do well. Come on. Let's make it the income of *The Liberty**.

Ayaori [*Laughs.*] [*Audience laugh.*] Then, do you mean Japan…

Duterte's G.S. A god. A god, you know? It's not a lie, you know?

---

* A Happy Science magazine featuring opinions on politics, economy, etc. Ayaori is its chief editor.

8　日本との「深い縁」を明かし、日本語で語り始める

ドゥテルテ守護霊　いやあ、英語で話さないとね、国際本部の収入にならないっていうから（会場笑）、頑張ってるんだよ。

綾織　（笑）

ドゥテルテ守護霊　もう苦しいよ。もう日本語でもいいよ。「もういいかげんにしろよ」って言いたいわけよ（会場笑）、ね？
　もう、日本の政治に腹立ってんの。分かる？　（綾織に）まあ、日本語に変えたら君、活躍できる。頑張れ。月刊「ザ・リバティ」（注）の収入に変えよう。

綾織　（笑）（会場笑）ということは、日本に……。

ドゥテルテ守護霊　ゴッドでしょ？　ゴッドでしょ？　嘘じゃないでしょ？

(注) 幸福の科学グループの書店売りオピニオン雑誌。綾織はその編集長。

Ayaori You are right.

Duterte's G.S. Yeah, a god. I have a shrine. A god. Yeah.

9 Regain the Spirit of Meiji and Stand Up, Japan

He complains about the emperor's abdication problem

Ayaori The thing you expect the most from Japan is military…

Duterte's G.S. Be independent. Independence! Yeah. I cannot forgive the corruption since Emperor Showa.

Ayaori Corruption?

綾織　その通りですね。

ドゥテルテ守護霊　うん、ゴッドだ。神社を持ってるもん。ゴッドだよ。うん。

9　日本は「明治の気概」を取り戻し立ち上がれ

天皇の「生前退位(せいぜんたいい)」問題に苦言を呈(てい)するドゥテルテ守護霊

綾織　日本にいちばん期待していることは、やはり、軍事的に……。

ドゥテルテ守護霊　独立しなさい、独立を！　うん。昭和天皇以降の、この堕落(だらく)は許せん。

綾織　堕落している？

Duterte's G.S. Abdication of the emperor*? I cannot forgive. It must be the end. The end of the Imperial Family.

Ayaori Ah, so you cannot forgive abdication?

Duterte's G.S. The Imperial Family will perish.

Ayaori I see. Ah.

Duterte's G.S. So, I cannot forgive. No.

Ayaori Do you mean that the abdication itself is not a good thing?

---

* On Jul. 13, 2016, Japanese media outlets reported that His Imperial Majesty Akihito showed his intention to the Imperial Household Agency that he wished to abdicate the title, while alive, to the crown prince. On Aug. 8, the emperor's video message was broadcasted on television. Currently, regarding the legislation that will allow for early abdication, the government is discussing how they can establish special measures laws to accept early abdication for one generation without revising the Imperial House Act.

ドゥテルテ守護霊　天皇の「生前退位」？（注）許せんよ。やっぱり、これはもう終わるよ。皇室が終わってしまう、これでは。

　綾織　あっ、「生前退位」自体が許せないですか。

　ドゥテルテ守護霊　もう皇室、滅びるよ、これね。

　綾織　ほう。

　ドゥテルテ守護霊　だから、これはもう、やっぱり許せんよ。

　綾織　退位されるということ自体が、よくないことですか。

　（注）2016年7月13日、「天皇陛下が、天皇の位を生前に皇太子殿下に譲る『生前退位』のご意向を宮内庁関係者に示されている」との報道が出、8月8日には天皇陛下の「お言葉」のビデオメッセージがテレビ等で放映された。現在、生前退位を可能にする法整備に関して、政府は「皇室典範の改正はせず、一代に限って退位を認める特措法を制定する」方向で調整に入っている。

Duterte's G.S. It's not good. The Imperial Family will perish. Yeah, yeah. They will perish. They can do anything freely.

Oikawa They are trying to cover that by a special measures law, but is it not good?

Duterte's G.S. No, no, no. You know… Ah, I'm speaking Japanese. I guess it cannot be helped.

Ayaori [*Laughs.*] [*Audience laugh.*]

Duterte's G.S. It cannot be helped because you found out.

You know, letting the emperor step down and Mr. Abe extends his term. It's unforgivable. I cannot forgive this kind of thing as a subject of the emperor. It's not good.

ドゥテルテ守護霊　よくない。これ、皇室、滅びるよ。うん、うん。これ滅びに至る。そんなん、もう自由にできるもん。

及川　特措法で対処しようとしてますけど、それも駄目？

ドゥテルテ守護霊　んな、駄目よ。駄目、駄目です。あんなん。あ、もう、日本語になっちゃった。もうしょうがない。

綾織　（笑）（会場笑）

ドゥテルテ守護霊　ばれたから、しょうがない。

　あのね、だいたいね、天皇を退位させといてね、安倍さんだけ任期を延ばそうなんてね、こんなの許しがたいよ。あんなの、臣下の礼としては許せないことですよ。これは駄目です。

Ayaori But this is the will of His Imperial Majesty.

Duterte's G.S. His will is not good.

Ayaori Not good?

Duterte's G.S. He must not have his own will.

Ayaori Ah, he must not have his own will?

Duterte's G.S. People above the clouds must not have a will.

Ayaori Oh, oh.

Duterte's G.S. Yeah, yeah. I educated Emperor Showa so much. It's too sad.

Oikawa The present emperor repeatedly said "personal

綾織　ただ、これは天皇陛下のご意志でいらっしゃいますので……。

ドゥテルテ守護霊　ご意志が駄目なのよ。

綾織　それが……駄目なんですか。

ドゥテルテ守護霊　ご意志は持ってはいけないのよ。

綾織　持ってはいけない？

ドゥテルテ守護霊　うん。〝雲の上の人〟は持ってはいけないんです。

綾織　おお、おお。

ドゥテルテ守護霊　うん、うん。だから、私がせっかく昭和天皇をあそこまで育てたのにね。残念すぎるからね。

及川　（今上天皇は）盛んに、「個人的意見」と言われてい

opinion," but it's not allowed?

Duterte's G.S. He must not say his opinion. It's a political opinion, you know? He is the fundamental character of Japan. He must not speak. He must not speak too much. It's not good at all. It will leave a risk for the next generation. Will the next one be the last or not? It depends.

Ayaori Hmm.

Duterte's G.S. Hmm. It was revealed. And I was doing my best to speak in my poor English [*pounds table*] [*audience laugh*].

Ill words are "to teach the samurai spirit to Japan"

Ayaori Time is almost up, but what are you expecting from Japan right now in particular?

ましたけど、それは許されない？

ドゥテルテ守護霊　意見を言っちゃいけない。政治的意見だよ、やっぱりね。だから、「国体」なんだからね。「国体」はしゃべったらいけない。余計なことはね。そんなのは絶対駄目。もう次の代にリスクを負わせるから、あれは。うん。次の代で終わるかどうか、かかってくるよ。

綾織　うーん。

ドゥテルテ守護霊　まあ、ばれちゃったじゃないか。せっかく（机を叩く）（会場笑）、あの、頑張って下手な英語しゃべってるの……。

暴言の真意は「日本に武士の気概を教えるため」

綾織　今の日本に特に望んでいることというのは、何でしょうか。

9 Regain the Spirit of Meiji and Stand Up, Japan

Duterte's G.S. Please regain the Meiji spirit. Of course. Yeah! It's the only way. So, I came here all the way from the Philippines to Japan and I'm telling you to become strong. They are doing something stupid in Okinawa, so I came to say my opinion on behalf of you from the Philippines. To America, I said, "Obama, go to Hell." I spoke ill of him. So, I'm teaching the samurai spirit to the Japanese people…

Ayaori I see. [*Laughs.*] So, that was a samurai. [*Laughs.*]

Duterte's G.S. …"You are much stronger." Than the Philippines. Even the Philippines can say something like that, so speak out more. I want to say so.

Ayaori So, even if you receive a lot of money from China, which you said was a rental fee, ultimately, "Japan will solve the issue for us" is your true thought, right?

9 日本は「明治の気概」を取り戻し立ち上がれ

ドゥテルテ守護霊 やっぱりね、もう「明治の気概」を取り戻してくださいよ。うん！ それしかない。だから、私はわざわざフィリピンから言いにきてんだからさあ。これ、しっかりしろって、日本に来て、言ってきてるんだから。沖縄なんかでグチャグチャやってるから、フィリピンのほうから、代わりにちょっと意見を言ってるわけでしょう。アメリカに対して、「オバマは地獄に堕（お）ちろ」とか言って罵（ののし）ってだね、日本人に「武士の気概」を教えているわけよ。

綾織 なるほど（笑）。武士なんですね、あれは（笑）。

ドゥテルテ守護霊 「お前たちはもっと強いだろうが」って。フィリピンよりも。フィリピンでこのぐらいのこと言えるんだから、もっと頑張って言えということだな。

綾織 ということは、中国からたくさんお金をもらっても、〝レンタル料〟という話でしたけれども、最終的に、日本が何とかしてくれるというのが本心なんですね。

Duterte's G.S. You know, Japan will definitely stand up. You know, Japan is contained by America's "cap in the bottle"* logic, so you must remove it.

Ayaori OK. Ah, yeah.

Duterte's G.S. You must definitely remove it. And establish religious value and protect by yourself. Also, contribute to the people of Asia. That is Japan's duty. Surely. You must turn that around. It was wrong after World War II, so you must return it to the original position. So, I'm supporting you from the Philippines now. So, you know…

Oikawa Does the spirit of Meiji period include religious policies?

Duterte's G.S. Yeah, of course.

---

* The way of thinking that symbolizes Japanese rearmament and militarization as "coming out of a bottle" and the U.S. forces in Japan as the "cap" that prevents them from doing so.

9　日本は「明治の気概」を取り戻し立ち上がれ

ドゥテルテ守護霊　いやあ、日本はね、絶対立ち上がるよ。だから、アメリカの「瓶の蓋理論」（注）で、アメリカに封じ込められているの、これ取らなきゃ駄目だよ。

綾織　ああ、はい。

ドゥテルテ守護霊　絶対駄目だよ。それで、やっぱり宗教を立てて、ちゃんと防衛して、それからアジアの人々のために尽くす。これが日本の本分。間違いない。うん。戦後引っくり返ってたから、ここを絶対、元に戻さなきゃいけない。それで、フィリピンから応援してんだから、今は。だから……。

及川　「明治の気概」というのは、宗教政策も入るわけですね。

ドゥテルテ守護霊　もちろんそれはあるよなあ。

（注）日本の再軍備・軍国主義化を「日本が瓶のなかから出てくる」ことにたとえ、在日米軍はそれを防ぐ「瓶の蓋」であるとする考え方。

177

You say I killed more than one thousand several hundred drug addicts or drug dealers, but do you know how many people were killed at 203 Hill*? I don't care about it at all.

I will do anything for righteousness. First, I will improve the safety in the Philippines, and we can attract companies from overseas. No one will come to a dangerous place. Not at all.

And they are investing a lot into China, so we have to let them shift their investments next. In order to do that, we need to make a safe country in Southeast Asia. That's what I'm thinking right now. So, don't think badly of me. OK? Do you understand?

Oikawa I understood very well.

---

* The Siege of Port Arthur during the Russo-Japanese War, where Maresuke Nogi served as the commander, saw casualties of about 60,000 Japanese and 46,000 Russian soldiers. Nogi himself lost two of his sons in this war.

9　日本は「明治の気概」を取り戻し立ち上がれ

　だから、今はあんたがたが、この千何百人かぐらい麻薬患者を殺したとか、薬(ヤク)の売人を殺したとか言ってるけど、そんなもん、二〇三高地(にまるさんこうち)で何万人殺したと思ってるの？（注）何とも思ってないよ、そんなのね。

　だからね、正しいことのためにはね、何(なん)ぼでもやりますよ。それはもう。まずはフィリピンの治安をよくしてだね、海外から誘致できるようにしなきゃいけないわけよ。治安が悪かったら来ないからね、全然。

　だから、今中国にいっぱい投資してるからさ、あの投資をちょっと移動させなきゃいけない、次ね。そのためには、東南アジアにも治安のいい国をつくらなきゃいけないわけよ。それを考えてるんで。ええ、そんなに悪く思わないでくださいね。うん？　分かる？

及川　よく分かりました。

　　（注）乃木希典が司令官をつとめた日露戦争の「旅順攻囲戦」では、日本軍の死傷者は約６万名、ロシア軍の死傷者は約４万６千名であった。乃木自身も、二人の息子を日露戦争で亡くしている。

179

Suggesting the Greater East Asia Co-Prosperity Sphere to Japan from a foreign country

Duterte's G.S. OK? You understand that I'm a god. A small one, but a god. Surely.

Ayaori There is something I want to ask you about. You said it would be OK with Mr. Trump, but it could be Ms. Hillary. Very likely.

Duterte's G.S. For now, yeah. If America wants to decline, then it's OK. It will decline. If Ms. Hillary wins, she will try to keep Japan and the Philippines on a leash like a dog, but America will get weaker, so in the end, the leash will come off. So, in the end, they will become independent. It's the same thing.

So, we must make the Asian region stronger. The EU will break up next. Yeah. So, we must make Asia stronger. We should control China and India well and create a prosperity area of Asia. The Greater East Asia

9 日本は「明治の気概」を取り戻し立ち上がれ

外国から日本に「大東亜共栄圏」を提案している

ドゥテルテ守護霊　ね？　ゴッドだっていうこと分かったね？　まあ、小さいけどゴッドだ。間違いなくね。

綾織　ちょっと一つ気になるのは、「トランプさんだったら、それなりにいいでしょう」ということだったんですけども、ヒラリーさんになる可能性も、かなりあります。

ドゥテルテ守護霊　まあ、今んとこそうだね。アメリカが没落したければ、そうしたらいい。だから、没落するから。ヒラリーさんになったら、同じように日本もフィリピンも、犬の紐をつないだようにやろうとするだろうけど、力が落ちていくから、結局、紐はほどける。だから結局は独立するね。一緒だね。

　だから、アジア圏での強化を……、まあ、EUがまたほどけていくから、次ね。だから、アジアを強くしなきゃいけない。中国とインドを上手に操って、アジアの共栄圏をつくる。大東亜共栄圏は正しいのよ。正しかったのよ。だ

Co-Prosperity Sphere is correct. It was the right thing. I'm trying one more time to make Japan create that. From us. You don't listen unless you are told from foreign countries. I'm thinking of doing it from this side. So, inform people well through *The Liberty*. OK?

Ayaori OK.

Duterte's G.S. The Nogi Shrine is about to go down. It's about to be sold. It will be an apartment or something like that if it's left as it is.

Advice for the Happiness Realization Party and Happy Science

Oikawa Since this is a rare opportunity, could you give some words of advice for the Happiness Realization Party?

から、それを、もう一回、つくらせようと思ってる。こちらからね。外国から提案しないと、君たち聞かないからさ。こっちからやるつもりね。だから、「ザ・リバティ」が上手に伝えるの、いいかな？

綾織　そうですね。

ドゥテルテ守護霊　まあ、乃木神社が潰(つぶ)れそうだから、もう、これ、売られそう。マンションかなんかになりそうだから。このままだと。

幸福実現党と幸福の科学へのアドバイス

及川　せっかくの機会なので、幸福実現党について何か、お言葉をいただけますか。

Duterte's G.S. Ah, you know, mountains of dead people. Wonderful.

Oikawa [*Smiles wryly.*]

Duterte's G.S. It's wonderful, I think. Wonderful. It's wonderful. You are showing Nogi spirit. It's good! Good!

Don't give up. If you do it for 10 years, the world will change. Yeah. Surely. The Japanese mass media cannot stand more than 10 years. They will treat you fairly. Definitely.

They cannot just keep reporting Liberal Democratic Party versus the alliance of opposition parties. They are just gathering without policies. You are insisting the right thing, so if the mass media keep ignoring you for 10 years, they are "no longer human." OK? Osamu Dazai*, you know? It's no good.

---

* Osamu Dazai (1909-1948) is a Japanese writer. The book, *No Longer Human* is one of his popular novels.

ドゥテルテ守護霊　いやあ、屍累々、素晴らしい。

及川　（苦笑）

ドゥテルテ守護霊　うん。やっぱりね、素晴らしいと思うよ。素晴らしいと思う。うん、うん。それは素晴らしい。「乃木精神」を体現している。あれは、いい！　いい！
　諦めずにやりたまえ。10年やったら世界は変わる。間違いない。日本のマスコミも、10年以上はもう我慢できなくなるから、必ず、ちゃんと扱うようになるね。

　だって、「自民党 対 野党連合」？　こればっかり、もうやってられないじゃない。そんなのただの野合じゃん。それに対して、一言、ひとり正論を吐き続けてるのを、10年無視し続けたら、〝人間失格〟よ。ね？　太宰治よ（注）。だから、もう、これ駄目よ。

（注）太宰治（1909〜1948）は日本の小説家。『人間失格』は代表作の一つ。

So, keep going for three more years. Then, there will be more fans. There will be more fans, definitely. Don't be discouraged. It's OK. The way will surely open. There is railroad in front of you. There is. Now, we are trying to make up for Japan's failure. We will do it.

Oikawa Thank you very much.

Sakakibara This is a rare chance, and there's Happy Science activities in the Philippines, too.

Duterte's G.S. Go, go. Do more. Jesus is just a servant. You know, he's just a servant or a manager. He's a manager, so use him more.

Sakakibara Umm, OK. [*Laughs.*] Do you have any advice? We are spreading our teachings in Asia, too.

Duterte's G.S. We want Japan to be more cool.

Be cool. Show us the samurai spirit. Your indecisive attitude is miserable. Be a man and show us the heart of samurai! Then the Philippine people will be attracted! It must be like that. Japanese people must pull themselves together. I think so.

10 Underground Plans for a New Worldview

"I will take as much as I can from China"

Ayaori From what you said earlier, it sounded a bit cruel, but what's your vision for the Philippines besides killing bad people? [*Laughs.*]

Duterte's G.S. First, right morals should prevail in the

だから、もうあと３年頑張れ。そうしたら、ファンが増える。必ず増えるからさ。挫(くじ)けるな。大丈夫。必ず道が開ける。君たちの先には線路が引いてあるから、ちゃんと。うん。これはね、私たちはね、この日本の失敗っていうのを取り返そうとしてるから、今。必ずやる。

及川　まことにありがとうございます。

榊原　せっかくですので、ハッピー・サイエンスの活動をフィリピンでも行っておりますし。

ドゥテルテ守護霊　うーん、やれやれ。もっとやれ。イエスなんて僕なんだから。ただの僕(しもべ)なんだからさあ、〝番頭〟だよ。番頭さんだから、もっと使え。

榊原　あの……はい（笑）。何かアドバイスとかあればあと、アジアにも弘(ひろ)めていっておりますけども。

ドゥテルテ守護霊　やっぱり日本にね、もっとかっ

くなってほしい。やっぱり、日本の「侍精神」をもっと、パシーッと決めてほしいねえ。何か、この、グチュグチュグチュチュするのね、あれね、情けない。だから、やっぱりもっとパシーッと、男らしく、「武士の心」をパシーッと打ち出してくれたら、フィリピンの人は、しびれるねえ！それでなきゃいけないと思うねえ。うん。やっぱりね、ビシーッと締めないといけないと思うなあ。うーん。

10　新たな世界観のための　〝地下計画〟を語るドゥテルテ守護霊

中国からは「むしるだけ、むしってやる」

綾織　先ほどの話だと、ちょっと、若干凄惨な印象もあったんですけども、悪い人たちを「殺す」以外で（笑）、「フィリピンの国をこうしたい」というお気持ちは、どういうものがありますか。

ドゥテルテ守護霊　まず真っ当な道徳がね、通用する国に

Philippines. That's important. You need to raise the quality of people, or nothing can be built. If we don't raise the level of people and establish right morals, education will be meaningless. They will use it for bad things. We want to have good relations with Japan from now on and become more powerful. You are saying other Asian countries will be intruded by China, but it's in a bubble. I know that. I will take as much money as I can.

Ayaori Oh, then, right now…

Duterte's G.S. Yeah. I will take as much as I can. I didn't make a real promise. I just got the aid first.

Ayaori I see, I see.

Duterte's G.S. Yeah. I didn't say until when. It's like Islam. "As Allah wills."

しなきゃいけないから。それが第一です。先に民度(みんど)を上げなきゃね、何にも立たないですよ、この上に。民度をまず上げて、きちんとした「道徳」が立たなかったら、「教育」やってももう駄目ですから。悪いことのほうに使うようになるからね。「教育」やって。日本とは今後はうまくやって、力をつけるつもりだから。アジアの諸国、ほかの国々も中国にやられるとか言ってるけど、中国のはバブルだから、分かってるから。お金をむしるだけむしってやるつもりで。

綾織　あっ、じゃあ、今の時点で……。

ドゥテルテ守護霊　うん。むしるだけむしってやる。だから、本当の約束してないから。援助だけは先に取ってるから。

綾織　なるほど、なるほど。

ドゥテルテ守護霊　うん。「いつまで」と言ってない。そこだけはイスラム教みたいにね、「神の思(おぼ)し召しのままに」なんで。

Reformers will come from Asian countries based on the world plan by Happy Science

Oikawa So, then, are you aiming to become a great economic power?

Duterte's G.S. Yeah. But I'm not aiming just for the prosperity of one country. I'm thinking of making an Asian team. So, China just needs to change their system. No? Then, you can be better friends with them. Maybe. But don't be too weak before that. I think so. You need to stand firmly. It's not good for you to be chained by America.

So, you know, the UN? Their "winning countries" structure? It needs to break down. If not, there will be no resurrection of Japan. Yeah. So, the next move, I thought about it already. I thought about it well. We, for support, now, are in the neighbor countries. A reformer will appear from inside China.

10　新たな世界観のための〝地下計画〟を語るドゥテルテ守護霊

幸福の科学の「世界計画」のもと、アジア各地に改革者が出てくる

及川　では、かなり経済的な、経済大国を狙(ねら)っているんですか。

ドゥテルテ守護霊　うん。だからね、一国だけの繁栄を目指してるわけじゃないよ。アジアでチームを組んで、やろうと思ってる。中国は、体制が変わりゃいいんでしょ？ あなたがたはもうちょっと仲良くできるよ。たぶんね。ただ、その前は、あまり弱すぎてはいけないと思うよ。毅然とした態度が要るし、アメリカに鎖(くさり)で縛られてる状態では駄目ね。

　だから、国連の戦勝国体制は、やっぱり崩(くず)れてもらわないと困るねえ。こうしないと、日本の復活はないね、やっぱり。もう、次は考えてるから。ちゃんと考えてるから。だから、私らは応援のために、今、ちょっと、近隣に（生まれて）出てるんで。中国の内部からも「改革者」は出るから。

Ayaori Ah, really?

Duterte's G.S. Soon. Yeah. Coming.

Ayaori Is that a part of your plan?

Duterte's G.S. We will show you. A reformer is coming soon. We will turn things around. Over there.

So, outside and inside, both need to act together. And Japan needs leaders who can do that. Now, we are accumulating our power in the field of thoughts. And we will turn things around. We will surely create a powerful prosperity area in Asia one more time.

Ayaori OK. Also, a person who was Japanese in her past life but is Taiwanese in this life has become the president.*

Duterte's G.S. Right. So, we have a lot of underground plans. So, it's OK.

10 新たな世界観のための〝地下計画〟を語るドゥテルテ守護霊

綾織　あっ、そうですか。

ドゥテルテ守護霊　もうすぐ。うんうん。出る。

綾織　それも計画されている？

ドゥテルテ守護霊　（人材を）「出してある」から。出てくる。もうすぐ出てくるから。引っくり返すから。あっちも。

　だから、外と中と両方、呼応しなきゃいけないし、日本にもそれだけのリーダーは必要。今、思想的に、だから、力を溜めてるところだからね。これでね、引っくり返すから。うん。アジアはやっぱり一つの、「強力な共栄圏」をもう一回つくるから。

綾織　はい。台湾にも、日本出身の方が総統(そうとう)として生まれられたと。（注）

ドゥテルテ守護霊　そう。だから今、〝地下計画〟を、いっぱいほかにも持ってるから。大丈夫。

Ayaori Taiwan and the Philippines…

Duterte's G.S. Thailand also. We will definitely, definitely, definitely change.

Ayaori Who are the ones at the center of this plan? The Japanese Shinto gods?

Duterte's G.S. It's Happy Science! What are you saying?

Ayaori Is that so? [*Smiles wryly*.] Hmm.

10　新たな世界観のための〝地下計画〟を語るドゥテルテ守護霊

綾織　台湾、フィリピンもそうで……。

ドゥテルテ守護霊　タイも必ず、必ず、必ず変えます。

綾織　それを中心的に計画されている方というのは、日本の神々のなかで、そういう計画をされてるんでしょうか。

ドゥテルテ守護霊　幸福の科学がやってんじゃないの！ 何を言ってるの。

綾織　ああ、そうなんですか（苦笑）。ほう。

（注）2016年2月7日、1月16日投開票の台湾総統選挙で圧勝した蔡英文氏の守護霊霊言を収録した。同霊言のなかで、蔡英文氏の過去世は「東洋のルソー」と呼ばれた中江兆民であることが明らかにされた。『緊急・守護霊インタビュー　台湾新総統　蔡英文の未来戦略』（幸福の科学出版刊）参照。

★ On Feb. 7, 2016, Happy Science recorded a spiritual interview with the guardian spirit of Tsai Ing-wen, who won the Taiwanese presidential election on Jan. 16 by a landslide. In the interview, it was revealed that her past life was Chomin Nakae, who was also known as "the Rousseau of the East." See *Kinkyu Shugorei Interview Taiwan Shin Soto Sai Eibun no Mirai Senryaku* [Urgent Spiritual Interview with the Guardian Spirit of New Taiwanese President –Future Strategy of Tsai Ing-wen–] (Tokyo: IRH Press, 2016).

Duterte's G.S. Here is the center. Here is the center of the world! Uh-huh. We are born based on that plan. We predicted Japan would lose in World War II, so we chose to be born again to rebuild after it.

Ayaori OK.

End the "winning countries" system of the UN and make a new worldview

Oikawa Is that why you criticize the UN so much?

Duterte's G.S. The UN is bad. I cannot allow them to continue. It's wrong if they think that continuing their "winning countries" system is justice. They are wrong. Germany is not treated fairly also. They are being deprived of their money from the EU, but they are not allowed leadership. It's a very slave-like situation, just like Japan. We must free them. So, we

ドゥテルテ守護霊 ここが中心だよ。ここが「世界の中心」なんだ！ 私たちはその計画のもとに出てるんだから。第二次大戦の敗戦を予想して、次の「戦後の再建」のために、もう、生まれてるわけだからさ。

綾織 はい。

国連の「戦勝国体質」を廃し、新たな世界観の構築を

及川 国連に対しての批判を、そうとう言われていましたが。

ドゥテルテ守護霊 国連は駄目ね。もうこれ以上続けるのは許せないね。やっぱり、「戦勝国体質」を続けることが正義っていうのは、それはおかしい。あれは絶対間違っているから。ドイツも不当に扱われすぎてるから、ＥＵで、金絞（しぼ）られるだけ絞られて、指導権をなかなか発揮できないでいて、非常に卑屈な状態は日本と一緒。これ、全部解放してやらないと、いけないね。だから、新しい世界観をつ

must make a new worldview.

I can do just one part only, but at least I will end American hegemony and make China powerless at the same time. I will do those at the same time. Withdrawal of American hegemony and making China weaker. At the same time. Japan must become the leader of Asia. It's the only way. Japan should be the leader of Asia and Oceania.

Japan should regain the spirit of 1970s and 1980s. That's important. America is losing its mission now. We need the next mission, Asia mission. You, Happy Science, must carry that.

You are building the foundation now. Maybe you are not getting anything in return now, but the longer it takes, the bigger the fruit will be in the future. It's very huge. So, the EU will get weaker little by little, but Germany will still be its center.

くらなきゃいけない。

　私ができるのは、一部だけどね。少なくとも、「アメリカの覇権を終わらせる」と同時に、「中国の牙も抜く」。同時に、やるから。アメリカの覇権撤退と中国の牙抜き、同時にやるから。もうアジアでは、日本がリーダーになるしかないと思う。アジア、オセアニアのリーダーは日本がなるべきだ。

　だから、一九七〇年代、八〇年代の気概をもう一回取り戻す。それが大事なことで、今、アメリカのミッションが見えなくなってきているからね。これは次のミッションが必要になってきた。アジア・ミッション、これを君たちが背負うことになっている。

　だから、君たちがやってることは今、〝基礎工事〟だけども、今は報われてないかもしれないけども、報われない時代が長ければ長いほど、先に待ってるものが大きいってことだね。すごく大きいものが待ってるから。ＥＵも少しずつ弱っていくと思うけど、やっぱりドイツ中心になるだろうけどね。

Problems of the mass media in the Japanese election system and in democracy

Oikawa You met with Mr. Abe this time. What was your real impression on him?

Duterte's G.S. No one else can replace him. [*Laughs.*] I guess so. It's sad. But there is a problem in the election system. The mass media are aiming to protect themselves. They want to keep the status quo. They want to keep the status quo, so they are working hard to get closer to the administration.

I don't think this is the correct way of democracy. The emperor said he will hand over the position, but they reported it as abdication. There is a difference between handing over and abdication. Abdication means he might be expelled. Handing over means he will become a retired emperor.

Ayaori True.

日本の選挙システムや民主主義における
マスコミの問題点

及川　そういう意味で、今回、安倍さんとお会いになられた本当の印象はどうなんでしょうか。

ドゥテルテ守護霊　まあ、……ほかに代わりがないって言ったら（笑）残念なことだね。選挙システムにちょっと問題があるんだろう。マスコミが、どうしても、自分たちの保身を目指してるからね。現状維持？したいからさ。現状は維持できるように、一生懸命政権に擦り寄ってる状態だよな。

　だから、正しい民主主義のあり方じゃないんじゃないかなあ。天皇陛下も、「生前譲位」と言ってたのに、「退位」って報道したのはマスコミだからね。譲位と退位は、違いがあるからね。退位だったらもう、追い出しじゃないですか。譲位だったら上皇になるっていうことだからね。

綾織　うーん。

Duterte's G.S. So, the current emperor said he will hand over the position meaning that he will become a retired emperor. But the mass media keep saying abdication. They kept saying that and brainwashed all the people. So, he has no choice but to resign. The mass media report that it's his will, so even though he says something in protest, it will be a political opinion.

That's the point. I might kill 20,000 or 30,000 people, but please be tolerant and welcome me. Do you know how many people I got killed at 203 Hill?

Ayaori [*Laughs.*]

Duterte's G.S. Maybe about 100,000. So many people died, but it was very important to win against Russia. That's how important it was. I don't want to lose what we did. Don't lose the prosperity, value systems, and culture of Japan that we worked hard to make, from the world. So, it's OK. Even if China tries to take in, it will be Japanized. The opposite will happen.

ドゥテルテ守護霊 今上天皇は、上皇になるつもりで、譲位とおっしゃっておられたのを、マスコミが「退位」「退位」って言うんで、いっぱい報道して、国民全部洗脳してしまったからね。これ、やめるしかないじゃないですかね、これだったら。御意志だって言うんで、いかなる抗弁をしても政治的な発言になるからね。

　まあ、そういうとこだ。まあ、２、３万人殺すかもしらんけど、君たち、寛容に迎えてくれ。二〇三高地で私は何人殺したと思ってるの。

綾織　（笑）

ドゥテルテ守護霊　10万ぐらい殺したかなあ。まあ、そのぐらい屍重ねてでもですね、ロシアに勝つってことは大きなことだったんですよ。せっかくやったことをね、やっぱり、失いたくないわねえ。せっかくつくった日本の繁栄と日本的価値観、文化は、世界から失われてはいけませんよ。だから、大丈夫。中国が飲み込もうとしても、逆に、中国が「日本化」しますから。

Heaven's plans to make China weaker

Ayaori I think it would be very difficult to make China weaker...

Duterte's G.S. We will do it. We will. It's OK. There is no mistake with Heaven's plans.

Ayaori Oh! I see.

Duterte's G.S. We have a detailed plan.

Ayaori So, you mean, it has been taken care of in many ways?

Duterte's G.S. Yeah, it has been taken care of. It's OK. Just carry out what you need to do and succeed in it. This is important.

Ayaori OK.

中国の「牙を抜く」天上界の計画とは

綾織 「中国の牙を抜く」というのは、なかなか難しいことであると思うんですけども……。

ドゥテルテ守護霊 やります。やります。大丈夫です。天上界の計画に漏れはございません。

綾織 あ！ なるほど。

ドゥテルテ守護霊 ちゃんと計画があります。

綾織 それは、いろんな手が、もうすでに打たれているわけですね。

ドゥテルテ守護霊 まあ、ちゃあんと手を打ってますから。大丈夫です。ただ、あなたがたは「あなたがたのやることを、ちゃんと貫いて、成功すること」が大事です。

綾織 はい。

Comments on the Northern Territories issue with Russia

Oikawa Mr. Abe will be meeting Mr. Putin in December, but what is your opinion on the issues with the Northern Territories?*

Duterte's G.S. Two islands will be returned if you negotiate. These two islands were a promise. Regarding the other two islands, you cannot get them back without a war. If not, you can get them back if Russia falls under a financial crisis, and asks us to buy them. Otherwise, the two islands won't come back. Tens of thousands of people are living on the islands.

Two islands will come back. Only around a thousand people live there. You can get them back if you negotiate well. Still, it's progress. I think it's

---

* In Dec. 2016, President Putin will visit Japan to hold talks with Prime Minister Abe at his hometown in Yamaguchi Prefecture. Many believe this will be a big opportunity for the talks to push negotiations on the Northern Territories.

ロシアとの北方領土問題に関するコメント

及川　これから安倍さんが、プーチンさんと12月に会いますが、ロシアとの「北方領土の問題」に関しては、どういうふうにご覧になっていますか。(注)

ドゥテルテ守護霊　まあ、二島は還るでしょうね、交渉すればね。二島は、もともとの約束だからね。「あとの二島は戦争で取り返さないかぎり還らない」っていうことでしょうけども。でなければ、ロシアがもっと経済的危機に陥って、「買ってくれ」と言ってくる場合には還ってくるでしょうけど、あとの二島はそのままでは還らないわね。万の単位の人が住んでるからね。

　だから、二島は還ってくるっしょ。人が住んでない、1000人ぐらいしかいないところのほうはね。あちらは還ってくるでしょうから、うまくやればね。でも、それでも前

（注）2016年12月上旬、プーチン大統領の来日と、安倍首相の地元・山口県での首脳会談が予定されている。会談は、北方領土交渉を進める大きな機会であるとの見方が多い。

better to make a peace treaty. So, it depends on the negotiation. If Putin and Trump can both do well with Japan and form a triangle, it will be good. Hmm.

"I am one of the founding gods of Japan"

Ayaori Is this your first time being born in a foreign country?

Duterte's G.S. Hmm? No, I have been, but most of the time, I was born in Japan. It's been mainly Japan, yeah. I am definitely one of the founding gods of Japan.

Ayaori Were you Masashige Kusunoki*?

Duterte's G.S. Yeah, maybe something like that.

進だから。平和条約、結んどいたほうがいいんじゃないの。あとは、これから、交渉次第だけどね。プーチン、トランプあたりが全部、日本とうまくトライアングル組めると、うまくいくんじゃないかな。

日本の草創の神の一柱であることを明言

綾織　海外にお生まれになったのは、初めてなんでしょうか。

ドゥテルテ守護霊　うん？　そんなことはないけど。まあ、主として日本だけどね。主として日本ではあるけど、「日本の草創の神」であることは間違いないけどね。

綾織　確か、楠木正成（くすのきまさしげ）さん（注）？

ドゥテルテ守護霊　うん、まあ、そういうのもあったかもしれない。

10 Underground Plans for a New Worldview

Ayaori Is there any other past lives you can tell us about?

Duterte's G.S. You don't know names other than the emperors. I was in ancient times, yeah.

Ayaori Were you a helper of an emperor…

Duterte's G.S. I have helped during the time when the Imperial Household was established.

Ayaori I see, I see.

綾織　それ以外で、もし何か、教えていただけるようなものがあれば。

ドゥテルテ守護霊　いや、天皇以外は知らないでしょう、君たち。まあ、昔の、何とかの尊(みこと)とかいう時代には、それは、いましたけどね、うん。

綾織　天皇や、天皇をお助けする立場の方……。

ドゥテルテ守護霊　皇室を確立する過程でね、役に立ったことは、あるわなあ。

綾織　なるほど。

（注）2013年に収録された霊言で乃木希典は、自身の過去世について「『七回生まれ変わっても、この国を護る』と言った人間だ」と言及しており、自刃に際して「七生報国」を誓った武将・楠木正成（1294？〜1336）であると思われる。『秋山真之の日本防衛論』（幸福実現党刊）第2章参照。

* In a spiritual interview recorded in 2013, Maresuke Nogi referred to his past life by saying, "I was the one who said, 'Even If I were reborn seven times, I will protect this country.'" It is thought that he was Commander Masashige Kusunoki (1294?~1336), who vowed unfailing devotion to his country upon his suicide by sword. See Chapter 2 in *Akiyama Saneyuki no Nihon Bouei Ron* [Saneyuki Akiyama's Defense Theory of Japan] (Tokyo: Happy Realization Party, 2010).

Oikawa Thank you for your time, in both Japanese and English...

Duterte's G.S. Your English was difficult.

Oikawa I'm sorry [*laughs*].

Duterte's G.S. OK, OK.

Oikawa Thank you very much.

Duterte's G.S. So, I might be called a mad dog or something like that, but please support me and that I heard the voice of a god was not a lie.

及川　今日は長時間にわたって、日本語と英語で……。

ドゥテルテ守護霊　いやあ、君のイングリッシュはむつかしかったよ。

及川　すみません（笑）。

ドゥテルテ守護霊　うん。うん。

及川　どうもありがとうございました。

ドゥテルテ守護霊　まあ、そういうことだから、私の、これから、なんか、〝マッド・ドッグ〟とか、いろいろ言われるんだろうけれども、まあ、援護してね。それでね、あの「神の声が聞こえた」っちゅうのは、嘘でなかったっちゅうことも。

Why does he pretend to be uncivilized unlike his past life as a great general?

Ayaori [*Laughs.*] So, are you just pretending to be uncivilized? You are not a rude person, originally.

Duterte's G.S. I get popular...

Ayaori Oh, really [*laughs*] [*audience laugh*].

Duterte's G.S. ...that way in the Philippines.

Ayaori Oh, so you're doing it for the Filipinos.

Duterte's G.S. Hmm, well, like Schwarzenegger. Like him. That is what I'm doing. In a similar way, you know? There are a lot of crimes in the Philippines and the people are bad. I must tighten it.

名将の生まれ変わりらしからぬ「野蛮な振る舞い」は何のため？

綾織　(笑)何か、野蛮に振る舞っているのは、やはり演技なんですか。そういう方ではないですよね。

ドゥテルテ守護霊　いやあ、やっぱり、人気出るのよ。

綾織　ああ、そうですか(笑)(会場笑)。

ドゥテルテ守護霊　フィリピンでは、それらしくやったほうが。

綾織　ああ、フィリピンの方々向けなんですね。

ドゥテルテ守護霊　いや、あのね、シュワルツネッガーの、なんかああいう感じ、やってるわけよ、こう、ダーッっと。あの感じね。分かる？　だから、犯罪があまり溢れててね、もうフィリピン人も、ほんと、駄目になってるのよ。これ、引き締めないといかんからさあ。

Ayaori I see.

Duterte's G.S. So, a scary person will appear…

Oikawa Isn't it about human rights or something?

Duterte's G.S. To be honest, I don't care about human rights at all because I am a god. It's OK, if final result is good. But the small, that Obama with small balls.

Ayaori & Oikawa [*Laughs.*]

Duterte's G.S. He doesn't have, in fact. I'm really angry with him. Hmm.

Ayaori Yeah, I understand your true thoughts.

Duterte's G.S. You do? This is a big news for *The Liberty*.

綾織　なるほど。

ドゥテルテ守護霊　怖いのが出てくる……。

及川　人権とか何とかって言うんじゃないんですよね。

ドゥテルテ守護霊　人権なんて、もう、神様だからそんなんどうでもいいわけよ、はっきり言えば。だから、最終的にいいほうに持っていけば、いいわけで。まあ、そら、ちっちゃい、オバマが小さい、キンタマ小さい、あれねえ。

綾織・及川　（笑）

ドゥテルテ守護霊　ないんじゃねえか、ほんとは。ほんと腹立つねえ。うーん。

綾織　はい。真意がよく分かりました。

ドゥテルテ守護霊　分かった？　だから、もうこれは、「ザ・リバティ」の特ダネよ。うん。

Ayaori Yeah, it's a really big scoop.

Duterte's G.S. So, half the income of this session goes to the International Headquarters [*audience laugh*]...

Sakakibara Thank you.

Duterte's G.S. Around half goes to *The Liberty*. It's just that...

Ayaori Thank you.

Duterte's G.S. You must give back something.

Oikawa Thank you for your time today.

Duterte's G.S. Ah, OK, OK.

Ayaori Thank you very much.

綾織　そうですね、もうほんとに、大特ダネです。

ドゥテルテ守護霊　だから、半分国際本部に収入は上がり……（会場笑）。

榊原　ありがとうございます。

ドゥテルテ守護霊　やや半分、「ザ・リバティ」にちょっとなんか……。

綾織　ありがとうございます。

ドゥテルテ守護霊　「お返し」しなきゃいかんねえ。

及川　今日は本当に長時間、まことにありがとうございました。

ドゥテルテ守護霊　ああ、はいはい。

綾織　ありがとうございました。

Sakakibara Thank you very much.

11 After the Spiritual Interview from the Guardian Spirit of Duterte

Ryuho Okawa [*Claps hands twice.*] I didn't expect this kind of conclusion. It is quite hard to disguise oneself.

Ayaori But he was quite a noble person.

Ryuho Okawa He really was.

Ayaori Quite a big difference…

Ryuho Okawa He was a prosecutor before. When people see him, they will think he is a gangster, for a moment.

榊原　ありがとうございます。

11　ドゥテルテ守護霊の霊言を終えて

大川隆法　（手を二回叩く）まったく予想外の展開でございました。なかなか、〝化ける〟のも大変でございますね。

綾織　非常に高潔な方でいらっしゃるので。

大川隆法　実は、そうでしたね。

綾織　もうかなり、ちょっとギャップがあるんです……。

大川隆法　でも、元検事だから。みんな、あれ見たら、〝ごろつき〟かと思うやんなあ、一瞬。

Ayaori [*Laughs.*] Yeah.

Ryuho Okawa But he was born into an upper class family in the Philippines and is the son of a lawyer, and became a prosecutor. So, he is just acting based on the rule of law. There is no death penalty in the Philippines. So, trials are meaningless, because drug dealers come back. And sometimes judges receive bribes and they become not guilty, so killing them seems to be most effective. Around his age, they were the ones that killed people, so that is why they can stand it. Japanese now don't have this kind of feeling.

It is not good to be too rude, but they are trying to tighten up. And since we are trying to become closer with Russia because Putin was Japanese*, we should also have a friendly relationship with the Philippines. Now we know what kind of person he is.

This is a scoop. Yes. Thank you.

綾織　（笑）そうです。

大川隆法　だけど、フィリピンの上流階級の、法律家の息子に生まれて、検事なんですからね。だから、法にのっとって、やってるつもりでいるらしいから。実際、フィリピンでは死刑がないから、裁判をやっても駄目なんです。薬(ヤク)の売人たちはみんな戻ってくるので。そのうちに買収されたりして無罪になるので、撃ち殺すのがいちばん効果があるらしい。そのへんは、人を殺した世代だから耐えられるんでしょうね。今の日本人が、ちょっと離れすぎているんでしょうね。

　あまり野蛮でないほうがいいとは思いますけれども、引き締めようとしているのは確かなようなので。「プーチンが日本人だ」ということで（注）、今、うちも接近を図っているなら、「ここも、いちおう、友好国に入れてやらなければいけないらしいな」ということで。本心が分かりました。
　これはスクープですね。はい。ありがとうございました。

11 After the Spiritual Interview from the Guardian Spirit of Duterte

Ayaori Thank you very much.

Ryuho Okawa The presidency is tough work.

綾織　ありがとうございます。

大川隆法　大統領ってのは、大変だ。

（注）以前の霊言で、プーチン大統領は過去世で、奈良の大仏を建立した聖武天皇、室町幕府第８代将軍・足利義政、江戸幕府第８代将軍・徳川吉宗として転生していたことが判明している。『ロシア・プーチン新大統領と帝国の未来』（幸福実現党刊）、『プーチン大統領の新・守護霊メッセージ』（幸福の科学出版刊）参照。

* In his previous spiritual interviews, it was revealed that President Putin's past lives consisted of Emperor Shomu who erected the Great Statue of Buddha in Nara, the eighth Muromachi Shogunate Yoshimasa Ashikaga, and the eighth Edo Shogunate Yoshimune Tokugawa. See *President Putin and the Future of Russia* (Tokyo: HS Press, 2012) and *A New Message from Vladimir Putin* (Tokyo: HS Press, 2014).

『ドゥテルテ フィリピン大統領 守護霊メッセージ』
大川隆法著作関連書籍

『フィリピン巨大台風の霊的真相を探る』
(幸福の科学出版刊)
『緊急・守護霊インタビュー 台湾新総統
蔡英文の未来戦略』(同)
『秋山真之の日本防衛論』(幸福実現党刊)
『ロシア・プーチン新大統領と帝国の未来』(同)
『プーチン大統領の新・守護霊メッセージ』
(幸福の科学出版刊)

ドゥテルテ フィリピン大統領 守護霊メッセージ

2016年11月4日 初版第1刷

著　者　　大　川　隆　法
発行所　　幸福の科学出版株式会社

〒107-0052 東京都港区赤坂2丁目10番14号
TEL(03) 5573-7700
http://www.irhpress.co.jp/

印刷・製本　　株式会社 研文社

落丁・乱丁本はおとりかえいたします
©Ryuho Okawa 2016. Printed in Japan. 検印省略
ISBN 978-4-86395-857-9 C0030
Photo：Geoscience／EPA＝時事／AFP＝時事

大川隆法ベストセラーズ・英語説法&世界の指導者の本心

Power to the Future
未来に力を

英語説法集 日本語訳付き

予断を許さない日本の国防危機。混迷を極める世界情勢の行方――。ワールド・ティーチャーが英語で語った、この国と世界の進むべき道とは。

1,400円

ヘンリー・キッシンジャー博士 7つの近未来予言

英語霊言 日本語訳付き

米大統領選、北朝鮮の核、米中覇権戦争、イスラム問題、EU危機など、いま世界が抱える7つの問題に対し、国際政治学の権威が大胆に予測！

1,500円

アメリカ合衆国建国の父 ジョージ・ワシントンの霊言

英語霊言 日本語訳付き

人種差別問題、経済対策、そして対中・対露戦略――。初代大統領が考える、"強いアメリカ"復活の条件。

1,400円

幸福の科学出版

大川隆法ベストセラーズ・世界の指導者の本心

キング牧師 天国からのメッセージ

アメリカの課題と夢

宗教対立とテロ、人種差別、貧困と移民問題、そして米大統領選の行方──。黒人解放運動に生涯を捧げたキング牧師から現代人へのメッセージ。

英語霊言 日本語訳付き

1,400円

守護霊インタビュー ドナルド・トランプ アメリカ復活への戦略

次期アメリカ大統領を狙う不動産王の知られざる素顔とは？ 過激な発言を繰り返しても支持率トップを走る「ドナルド旋風」の秘密に迫る！

英語霊言 日本語訳付き

1,400円

オバマ大統領の 新・守護霊メッセージ

日中韓問題、TPP交渉、ウクライナ問題、安倍首相への要望……。来日直前のオバマ大統領の本音に迫った、緊急守護霊インタビュー！

英語霊言 日本語訳付き

1,400円

※表示価格は本体価格(税別)です。

大川隆法「法シリーズ」・最新刊

正義の法
憎しみを超えて、愛を取れ

法シリーズ第22作

テロ事件、中東紛争、中国の軍拡――。
どうすれば世界から争いがなくなるのか。
あらゆる価値観の対立を超える
「正義」とは何か。
著者二千書目となる「法シリーズ」最新刊!

2,000円

第1章　神は沈黙していない――「学問的正義」を超える「真理」とは何か
第2章　宗教と唯物論の相克――人間の魂を設計したのは誰なのか
第3章　正しさからの発展――「正義」の観点から見た「政治と経済」
第4章　正義の原理
　　　　――「個人における正義」と「国家間における正義」の考え方
第5章　人類史の大転換――日本が世界のリーダーとなるために必要なこと
第6章　神の正義の樹立――今、世界に必要とされる「至高神」の教え

幸福の科学出版

大川隆法シリーズ・最新刊

地球を救う正義とは何か
日本と世界が進むべき未来

【IS のテロ】【中国の覇権拡大】【北のミサイル発射】【英国の EU 離脱】【アベノミクス失速】解決する道はある。

1,500円

蓮如の霊言
宗教マーケティングとは何か

卓越した組織力と、類まれなる経営戦略——。小さかった浄土真宗を一代で百万人規模に発展させた"経営術"の真髄を、あの世から特別指南。

1,400円

国際政治学の現在(いま)

世界潮流の分析と予測
大川隆法・大川裕太共著

尖閣問題、北のミサイル実験、原発廃止論、そして沖縄からの米軍撤退運動——亡国の危機が迫る日本は、どんな未来を望むべきか。国際政治学の最新トピックス、その核心を鋭く分析する。

1,500円

※表示価格は本体価格(税別)です。

幸福の科学グループのご案内

宗教、教育、政治、出版などの活動を通じて、地球的ユートピアの実現を目指しています。

幸福の科学

1986年に立宗。信仰の対象は、地球系霊団の最高大霊、主エル・カンターレ。世界100カ国以上の国々に信者を持ち、全人類救済という尊い使命のもと、信者は、「愛」と「悟り」と「ユートピア建設」の教えの実践、伝道に励んでいます。

(2016年11月現在)

愛

幸福の科学の「愛」とは、与える愛です。これは、仏教の慈悲や布施の精神と同じことです。信者は、仏法真理をお伝えすることを通して、多くの方に幸福な人生を送っていただくための活動に励んでいます。

悟り

「悟り」とは、自らが仏の子であることを知るということです。教学や精神統一によって心を磨き、智慧を得て悩みを解決すると共に、天使・菩薩の境地を目指し、より多くの人を救える力を身につけていきます。

ユートピア建設

私たち人間は、地上に理想世界を建設するという尊い使命を持って生まれてきています。社会の悪を押しとどめ、善を推し進めるために、信者はさまざまな活動に積極的に参加しています。

海外支援・災害支援

国内外の世界で貧困や災害、心の病で苦しんでいる人々に対しては、現地メンバーや支援団体と連携して、物心両面にわたり、あらゆる手段で手を差し伸べています。

自殺を減らそうキャンペーン

年間約3万人の自殺者を減らすため、全国各地で街頭キャンペーンを展開しています。

公式サイト www.withyou-hs.net

ヘレンの会

ヘレン・ケラーを理想として活動する、ハンディキャップを持つ方とボランティアの会です。視聴覚障害者、肢体不自由な方々に仏法真理を学んでいただくための、さまざまなサポートをしています。

公式サイト www.helen-hs.net

INFORMATION

お近くの精舎・支部・拠点など、お問い合わせは、こちらまで！

幸福の科学サービスセンター
TEL. **03-5793-1727**（受付時間火〜金:10〜20時／土・日・祝日:10〜18時）
幸福の科学公式サイト **happy-science.jp**

幸福の科学グループの教育・人材養成事業

ハッピー・サイエンス・ユニバーシティ
Happy Science University

ハッピー・サイエンス・ユニバーシティとは

ハッピー・サイエンス・ユニバーシティ(HSU)は、大川隆法総裁が設立された「現代の松下村塾」であり、「日本発の本格私学」です。
建学の精神として「幸福の探究と新文明の創造」を掲げ、チャレンジ精神にあふれ、新時代を切り拓く人材の輩出を目指します。

学部のご案内

人間幸福学部
人間学を学び、新時代を切り拓くリーダーとなる

経営成功学部
企業や国家の繁栄を実現する、起業家精神あふれる人材となる

未来産業学部
新文明の源流を創造するチャレンジャーとなる

未来創造学部 （2016年4月開設）
時代を変え、未来を創る主役となる

政治家やジャーナリスト、ライター、俳優・タレントなどのスター、映画監督・脚本家などのクリエーター人材を育てます。 ※

※キャンパスは東京がメインとなり、2年制の短期特進課程も新設します（4年制の1年次は千葉です）。2017年3月までは、赤坂「ユートピア活動推進館」、2017年4月より東京都江東区（東西線東陽町駅近く）の新校舎「HSU未来創造・東京キャンパス」がキャンパスとなります。

住所 〒299-4325 千葉県長生郡長生村一松丙 4427-1
TEL.0475-32-7770

幸福の科学グループの教育・人材養成事業

教育

学校法人 幸福の科学学園

学校法人 幸福の科学学園は、幸福の科学の教育理念のもとにつくられた教育機関です。人間にとって最も大切な宗教教育の導入を通じて精神性を高めながら、ユートピア建設に貢献する人材輩出を目指しています。

幸福の科学学園

中学校・高等学校（那須本校）
2010年4月開校・栃木県那須郡（男女共学・全寮制）
TEL **0287-75-7777**
公式サイト **happy-science.ac.jp**

関西中学校・高等学校（関西校）
2013年4月開校・滋賀県大津市（男女共学・寮及び通学）
TEL **077-573-7774**
公式サイト **kansai.happy-science.ac.jp**

仏法真理塾「サクセスNo.1」 TEL **03-5750-0747**（東京本校）

小・中・高校生が、信仰教育を基礎にしながら、「勉強も『心の修行』」と考えて学んでいます。

不登校児支援スクール「ネバー・マインド」 TEL **03-5750-1741**
心の面からのアプローチを重視して、不登校の子供たちを支援しています。
また、障害児支援の「ユー・アー・エンゼル！」運動も行っています。

エンゼルプランV TEL **03-5750-0757**
幼少時からの心の教育を大切にして、信仰をベースにした幼児教育を行っています。

シニア・プラン21 TEL **03-6384-0778**
希望に満ちた生涯現役人生のために、年齢を問わず、多くの方が学んでいます。

NPO 活動支援

学校からのいじめ追放を目指し、さまざまな社会提言をしています。また、各地でのシンポジウムや学校への啓発ポスター掲示等に取り組む一般財団法人「いじめから子供を守ろうネットワーク」を支援しています。

公式サイト **mamoro.org**
ブログ **blog.mamoro.org**
相談窓口 **TEL.03-5719-2170**

幸福の科学グループ事業

幸福実現党

内憂外患(ないゆうがいかん)の国難に立ち向かうべく、2009年5月に幸福実現党を立党しました。創立者である大川隆法党総裁の精神的指導のもと、宗教だけでは解決できない問題に取り組み、幸福を具体化するための力になっています。

幸福実現党 釈量子サイト
shaku-ryoko.net
Twitter
釈量子@shakuryoko
で検索

党の機関紙
「幸福実現NEWS」

幸福実現党 党員募集中

あなたも幸福を実現する政治に参画しませんか。

○ 幸福実現党の理念と綱領、政策に賛同する18歳以上の方なら、どなたでも党員になることができます。
○ 党員の期間は、党費(年額 一般党員5,000円、学生党員2,000円)を入金された日から1年間となります。

党員になると

党員限定の機関紙が送付されます(学生党員の方にはメールにてお送りします)。申込書は、下記、幸福実現党公式サイトでダウンロードできます。

住所 〒107-0052
東京都港区赤坂2-10-8 6階
幸福実現党本部

TEL 03-6441-0754
FAX 03-6441-0764
公式サイト **hr-party.jp**
若者向け政治サイト **truthyouth.jp**

幸福の科学グループ事業

出版メディア事業

幸福の科学出版

大川隆法総裁の仏法真理の書を中心に、ビジネス、自己啓発、小説など、さまざまなジャンルの書籍・雑誌を出版しています。他にも、映画事業、文学・学術発展のための振興事業、テレビ・ラジオ番組の提供など、幸福の科学文化を広げる事業を行っています。

アー・ユー・ハッピー？
are-you-happy.com

ザ・リバティ
the-liberty.com

幸福の科学出版
TEL 03-5573-7700
公式サイト irhpress.co.jp

ザ・ファクト
マスコミが報道しない「事実」を世界に伝えるネット・オピニオン番組

ザ・ファクト 検索

ニュースター・プロダクション

ニュースター・プロダクション（株）は、新時代の"美しさ"を創造する芸能プロダクションです。2016年3月には、ニュースター・プロダクション製作映画「天使に"アイム・ファイン"」を公開しました。

公式サイト
newstarpro.co.jp

入会のご案内

あなたも、幸福の科学に集い、ほんとうの幸福を見つけてみませんか？

幸福の科学では、大川隆法総裁が説く仏法真理をもとに、「どうすれば幸福になれるのか、また、他の人を幸福にできるのか」を学び、実践しています。

入会

大川隆法総裁の教えを信じ、学ぼうとする方なら、どなたでも入会できます。入会された方には、『入会版「正心法語」』が授与されます。（入会の奉納は1,000円目安です）

ネットでも入会できます。詳しくは、下記URLへ。
happy-science.jp/joinus

三帰誓願

仏弟子としてさらに信仰を深めたい方は、仏・法・僧の三宝への帰依を誓う「三帰誓願式」を受けることができます。三帰誓願者には、『仏説・正心法語』『祈願文①』『祈願文②』『エル・カンターレへの祈り』が授与されます。

植福の会

植福は、ユートピア建設のために、自分の富を差し出す尊い布施の行為です。布施の機会として、毎月1口1,000円からお申込みいただける、「植福の会」がございます。

ご希望の方には、幸福の科学の小冊子（毎月1回）をお送りいたします。詳しくは、下記の電話番号までお問い合わせください。

月刊「幸福の科学」　ザ・伝道

ヤング・ブッダ　ヘルメス・エンゼルズ

INFORMATION

幸福の科学サービスセンター
TEL. 03-5793-1727（受付時間 火〜金：10〜20時／土・日・祝日：10〜18時）
幸福の科学 公式サイト **happy-science.jp**